CW01594033

mettle

BIBLE READING NOTES

TO INSPIRE COURAGE SPIRIT CHARACTER

yfc CWR

Published 2015 by CWR, Waverley Abbey House, Waverley Lane, Farnham, Surrey GU9 8EP, England. Registered Charity No. 294387. Registered Limited Company No. 1990308.

Mettle Bible-reading notes are produced in association with British Youth for Christ. British Youth for Christ is part of Youth for Christ International, a movement of youth evangelism organisations in over 100 countries of the world. Please visit www.yfci.org for the country nearest you.

The notes on 'The Trinity' and 'Friendship' were previously published in *Mettle* Jan–Apr 2012. The notes on 'Discipline' were previously published in *Mettle* May–Aug 2012, and 'Talent' in *Mettle* Sep–Dec 2012.

See back of book for list of National Distributors.

Concept development by YFC and CWR.
Editing, design and production by CWR.
Printed in England by The Linney Group.

CONTENTS

WELCOME TO mettle
COURAGE SPIRIT CHARACTER ...

HELLO! IT'S A new issue of *Mettle* and here's what you'll find in these pages. First up, our Core readings explore the majesty and mystery that is the Holy Trinity. God the Father, the Son and the Holy Spirit. How should our better understanding of each of them change the way we live and relate to God? We'll find out!

Then we've got three Hot Potatoes to sink our teeth into. We'll unpack what true, godly friendship looks like, and get questioning why we need discipline as we follow God – and why it's really good for us. Finally, we've got the exciting topic of talent. No matter how talented or untalented you feel, the Bible tells us that we are *all* gifted in some way. So let's look at how we can first discover our own talents, then think about how we can use and develop these God-given gifts!

Enjoy!

The *Mettle* Team

FRI 1 JAN

READ:
1 PETER 1:1–9

KEY VERSE
V2

'God the Father ... the Spirit ... Jesus Christ'

THE TRINITY PT1

HAPPY NEW YEAR! It's a brand new year and a brand new issue of *Mettle*! In these core topic sections we're going to be exploring the Trinity, which is both key to our relationship with God and a bit of a mystery!

So what is the Trinity? Or, perhaps a better question would be, *who* is the Trinity? The answer is God the Father, God the Son and God the Holy Spirit. Three separate Persons who together make up one God.

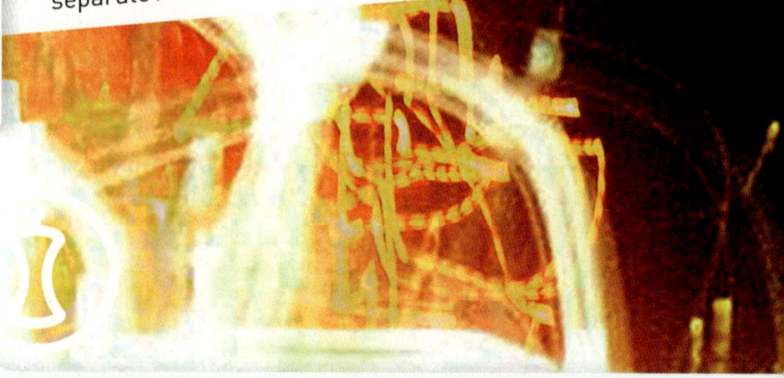

We'll find out more about each of them in these notes, but here's a quick introduction. God the Father is our Creator and Father in heaven. He is also the Father of Jesus (as we read in verse 3). Jesus, the Father's Son, came to earth as both fully human and fully God to die for our sins and defeat death. He then returned to heaven and left His followers (that includes us!) His Spirit – the Holy Spirit. The Spirit is God living in us.

All three were around before the beginning of time, all three were present during the creation of the world and all three will live on forever. To understand the God we worship, follow and love, we need to get to know every part of who He is.

CHALLENGE

Take some time out to write down the different names you already know about for the Father, Jesus and the Spirit (eg Creator, Saviour, Helper). Read through your list and put them all together in one big list (not three different ones). This may help with understanding the unity and harmony of the Trinity.

WEEKEND
2/3 JAN

READ:
MARK 1:9–11

KEY VERSE v10

'he saw heaven being torn open and the Spirit descending on him like a dove.'

GOD THE FATHER, God the Son and God the Holy Spirit. It's a weird concept to get your head around, isn't it? It's a mystery and will remain a mystery to humans this side of heaven. However, there are things about the Trinity we can begin to look into and understand.

The Bible is full of examples of this Triune (Three Person) God. Today's passage visibly and audibly reveals the Trinity working in perfect harmony. The Son, in obedience to the Father, is baptised in the River Jordan. As He comes out of the water, the Holy Spirit descends upon Jesus like a dove. He hears the voice of the Father in heaven saying, 'You are my dearly loved Son, and you bring me great joy.'

How do we explain the Christian doctrine that is 'the Trinity'? How can there be three in one? A simple example we can use is the mathematical illustration of 1x1x1=1. Here, the value of each independent number is 1 and the value of the multiplied numbers is 1. All are of equal value, yet when all are multiplied they still add up to 1. The Trinity makes the Christian faith completely unique. We worship a God who is one and yet three entities. This reveals to us something very key about God – that our God is a God of relationship.

THINK

Do you treat each member of the Trinity with equal value and respect? Is one Person of the Trinity easier to relate to than another? Who do you need to get to know more over time in order to have a deeper relationship with God?

MON 4 JAN

READ:
EPHESIANS 3:14–4:6

KEY VERSE V19

'know this love that surpasses knowledge – that you may be filled to the measure of all the fullness of God.'

WHEN PEOPLE GET married, it's often said that 'two become one'. In the unity and harmony of marriage, two separate people are joined together to make one couple.

Here, in Paul's letter to the Ephesians, we see the wonderful unity and harmony of the Trinity. They are three separate Persons yet they are still one God. It is wonderful to see how Paul embraces this Triune God in his prayer to the Ephesians. This great and mighty God is so awesome that Paul can do nothing more than kneel in worship before Him. He prays that the Ephesians may be strengthened by the Spirit; that the Spirit may give them the power to live for God every day and to be a disciple and follower of Christ. Finally, Paul prays that Christ may dwell deeply in their hearts.

Paul wants us to understand this amazing love of God in its immeasurable dimensions: its width, its depth, its length and its height. This love for mankind is just awesome! The Trinity is a living, vibrant relationship and we can be caught up in it as we live to serve a living, dynamic Almighty God.

PRAY

God, You are amazing. Please help me to understand the Trinity in a better way, to learn how Your relationship as Father, Son and Holy Spirit can affect my understanding of how to worship You, serve You and pray to You. Amen.

READ: JOHN 3:16

TUES 5 JAN

KEY VERSE v16

'For God so loved the world that he gave his one and only Son'

MORE ON GOD'S love today! Our reading, John 3:16, is probably one of the most well-known Bible verses and that's because it is so fundamental to what we believe as Christians.

Here we see a God who loves. He loves the world so much that He gave Himself, His one and only Son, to offer eternal life to you and me. This verse clearly shows us that our God is a God of relationship. Not only is God longing for a relationship with us – He's also a God who *is* relationship. He is in relationship with Himself as the Trinity.

Because of the Fall (Adam and Eve's disobedience), sin entered into the human race, causing a great divide between us and God. But God's longing for relationship with us inspired His rescue plan. His Son would bear the weight of the whole world's sin and atone for it on the cross. It is only through Jesus' death that we are brought into a right relationship with the Father, and receive the Holy Spirit to live in us. We no longer look forward to an eternity without God, but look forward to living with Him forever. What a fantastic gift!

PRAY

Thank You, Father, for giving Your one and only Son to die on the cross so that, through Him, we may enjoy relationship with You on earth now, and look forward to an eternity shared with You. Amen.

WED 6 JAN

READ:
HAGGAI 2:1–9

KEY VERSE v5

'my Spirit remains among you. Do not fear.'

IN THE OLD Testament, before Jesus' life, death and resurrection, the Holy Spirit acted like an agent of God, empowering specific people at a specific time, to do God's will. Here in today's reading we read a promise that the Spirit will remain with the nation of Israel – He will not just be with one or two *and* He will never leave.

Haggai records the Israelites' return from exile; their former cities are in ruin, their culture erased and their religion forgotten. As they begin to rebuild their nation, God promises that He'll remain with them just as He did when they crossed the Red Sea hundreds of years before, seeking the promised land.

From the very early days of Abraham and Isaac, God had chosen these people to represent Him to other nations. They often got it wrong and turned away from His rules for life, yet God continued to remain with them by His Spirit. When we turn our back on God, it is His Holy Spirit who remains with us and draws us back into relationship with Him.

CHALLENGE

Discuss with your friends how you have all seen God remaining with you through the good times and the bad. Listen to each other's testimonies and spend time thanking the Holy Spirit for His faithfulness.

READ: DEUTERONOMY 6:1–19

KEY VERSE V4

'the LORD our God, the LORD is one.'

IN TODAY'S PASSAGE we see Moses, towards the end of his life, preaching to the people of Israel before they enter the promised land. Moses wants these ex-slaves of Egypt to understand who their God is. The words of our key verse today are the words of the Jewish Shema, recited by devout Jews twice a day to ensure that they remember how different their God is from other gods.

In the last few days we have read about God's love and longing for relationship with us. Today we read that God is a 'jealous God' (v15), which means we can't love Him and love other 'gods' at the same time. These 'gods' may be a boyfriend/girlfriend, football, fashion or money. Whatever we're spending most of our time, energy and affection on, that's our god. So let's respond to God's amazing, huge love for us with the love He deserves: 'Love the LORD your God with all your heart and with all your soul and with all your strength' (v5).

THINK

As we're coming to the end of a week and the beginning of the weekend, think about what you devote your spare time to. Where does all your energy and love go? What can you do to show God that you place Him above everything, loving Him with ALL your heart, ALL your soul and ALL your strength?

FRI 8 JAN

READ: MATTHEW 6:7–13

KEY VERSE V8

'for your Father knows what you need before you ask him.'

WHAT DO YOU need to maintain a good relationship? How about time, communication, trust, honesty and love? All these are important in keeping our earthly friendships together, yet what about our relationship with our heavenly Father?

Already we know that our Triune God is a God of relationship – not just within the Godhead, but also with us, His people. So we need to be communicating with Him constantly to keep maintaining and growing this amazing relationship with the Trinity.

Knowing that He would not be with His disciples for long, Jesus teaches them how to pray. First, He says, go into your room and close the door. God has a relationship with you individually. Of course there are times of corporate prayer in church or with friends, but prayer should also be lots of one-to-one time with God. Second, don't 'babble' on and on, using fancy words for the sake of it, but speak honestly from the heart. And finally, Jesus tells us that God knows what we need before we even ask! Let's talk to Him, knowing that He cares about every aspect of our lives.

PRAY

Pray to God now, knowing that you are talking to the Trinity. You communicate to the Father, through knowing the Son, by the power of the Holy Spirit. The Father understands everything that is going on in your life and knows exactly what you need.

WEEKEND 9/10 JAN

READ:
JOHN 15:1–17

KEY VERSE
V15

'Instead, I have called you friends, for everything that I learned from my Father I have made known to you.'

PT1 FRiENDSHiP

AS WE BEGIN to look at the topic of friendship, think about the people you would call your friends. What are they like? Are you alike or are you completely different? What made you want to be their friend in the first place? What memories do you share?

Relationships with friends can be some of the most rewarding relationships in your life. You may lose touch with some friends, but others may never leave you. And memories and experiences of these friendships in our younger years will help us to forge new ones during our adult life.

CONTINUED▸▸

CONTINUED»

Of course, friendship is not all a walk in the park! Sometimes friendships go wrong. A friendship can go through difficult times as well as rewarding times. Jesus' disciples would certainly agree with this. Jesus chose 12 young men to be His closest friends, to share all that He was with them: His heart, His life, His love and His sorrow. In true friendship we share all aspects of our lives, which leaves us open and vulnerable to the other person. This may be one reason why some of us find it hard to forge deep friendships.

During our time looking at friendships, we'll seek to understand: what makes a friendship either good or bad, what to do when friendship goes wrong, how to be a good friend and what it means to be friends with God.

PRAY

Lord God, thank You for Your friendship and love for me. Help me to see what good friendship is and to appreciate it with a thankful heart. Amen.

READ:
PROVERBS 17:14–22

KEY VERSE v17

'A friend loves at all times, and a brother is born for a time of adversity.'

WHEN I WAS 13, my dad became really ill and had to give up work. He tried to go back to work but ended up in hospital again and was told off by the doctors. He was told that he would never be able to work again and he needed to start taking it easy. When someone loses their job, finances in the home become difficult to manage. The things you once took for granted now become luxuries. Inevitably, the lack of finances eventually started to become evident in the lack of the latest fashions in my wardrobe. The teasing started, and some so-called friends even stopped hanging around with me because of what I was wearing.

These friends were not true friends. They were only happy to be seen with the girls who looked good or wore fashionable clothes. It hurt at the time, but looking back I was happy to have other true friends around me. A true friend is one who sticks with you, no matter what the circumstances: his or her love is not dependent on things going well.

CHALLENGE

Take an honest look at what type of friend you are. Are you willing to stick by people no matter what? Or do you distance yourself when a friend is struggling?

TUES 12 JAN

READ: COLOSSIANS 3:7–12

KEY VERSE v12

'clothe yourselves with compassion, kindness, humility, gentleness and patience.'

HOW WOULD YOU describe yourself? If you were to list the qualities you show, would your list look like the one in our key verse today? Perhaps you have different qualities that are equally important. In any case, our character says something about us. It tells those around us what type of person we are. When we were making friends with someone, we probably saw a glimpse of their character, decided 'I like them', and so the friendship began. I would want to be a friend with someone who showed the qualities mentioned in today's reading. I think that I could have confidence in someone with these qualities and would be able to trust them.

What's more important, though, is whether I want to be the type of friend who shows qualities like these. The Bible tells us to clothe ourselves with these qualities. Why? Well, when we clothe ourselves, others see that clothing. In the same way God wants these qualities to be evident in our lives so that others can see them. As we allow the Holy Spirit to work in us, we'll become more like Jesus – and these qualities will grow in us.

CHALLENGE

Try writing down a list of words that describe your character. When your friends spend time with you, what qualities do they see in you?

READ: COLOSSIANS 3:13–17

KEY VERSE v13

'Bear with each other and forgive one another if any of you has a grievance against someone.'

YESTERDAY WE THOUGHT about our character and the qualities we show. Today, let's consider the qualities our friends have – and also what we think they may lack! Our friends may have different qualities from us, which at times may be frustrating. For example, you might be a really honest person, yet your friend may struggle with telling little lies now and again, perhaps to develop a story and make it sound more interesting than it actually was. They may not see any problem in doing this. Does this make them a bad person?

If we're honest then we can all admit that we have our faults. And, sometimes, something we see as a fault in someone else might not be a fault at all – just something we don't like! What we consider important priorities in life may not be the same as another person's priorities. When this situation occurs, we could easily mistake this for a fault or a flaw in their character. In friendship we need to have the grace to allow them to be unique and to forgive any genuine faults they show. After all, we have our own faults, as well as our strange little habits!

THINK

Do any of your friends wind you up? Is this because of a genuine fault in them? If so, perhaps it's time to forgive them. If it's just because of a strange habit, ask God for grace to tolerate it!

THURS 14 JAN

READ:
1 SAMUEL 18:1–3; 19:1–7

KEY VERSE 18:3

'And Jonathan made a covenant with David because he loved him as himself.'

DAVID AND JONATHAN are one of the best pictures of a deep and abiding friendship that we find in the Old Testament. They protected and loved each other in all they did. In the NIV translation of our reading today it says that they were even 'one in spirit' (18:1). The hallmarks of their relationship were closeness and trust.

Saul was king and Jonathan was the king's son. When David was in danger as a consequence of Saul's jealousy and fear, Jonathan warned David and even went so far as to plead his case to his father. On many occasions it was because of Jonathan's intervention that David's life was spared. Putting his friendship above the king's orders could have cost Jonathan his life at times. But Jonathan's actions meant that David survived and went on to be one of the greatest kings ever, leading Israel into a period of prosperity and wholehearted worship of God.

PRAY

Dear Lord Jesus, You once said, 'There is no greater love than to lay down one's life for one's friends.' You laid down Your life for me so that I might have a relationship with God the Father. Thank You. Please show me how to be a true and good friend, like Jonathan was and You are. Amen.

READ: 1 SAMUEL 26:1–25

KEY VERSE v6

'"I'll go with you," said Abishai.'

KING SAUL'S JEALOUSY of David had got the better of him once again and he got his army together to seek David out and kill him. David knew where they were camping overnight and made a plan to show the king that he meant him no harm. David was to enter the enemy camp in the dead of night and take something from close to the king. This was to show him that he could have killed him but chose not to. (David knew that Saul was God's anointed king and he would not remove Saul from the throne without God's say-so.) This mission was going to be dangerous and David asked two of his closest allies to go with him. Abishai agreed. He risked his own life for David.

Now I'm not saying that we should risk our lives for our friends, but there are times when our friends need us to go out of our way to help them. For example, they may need us to help them through a broken relationship on the same night that we're invited to a party. Or a friend may need encouragement when others are bringing them down. If we help we can put ourselves in the firing line too. But this is an important part of what being a true friend is.

THINK

What sacrifices have you made in the past to help out a friend? Would you be prepared to stand up for your friends even if it meant that you could suffer too?

WEEKEND

16/17 JAN

READ:
ROMANS 5:1–11

KEY VERSE v11

'we also boast in God through our Lord Jesus Christ, through whom we have now received reconciliation.'

JESUS OFFERS US friendship. He offers us friendship not just with God the Son but also God the Father and God the Holy Spirit. We've been given the opportunity to have a wonderful relationship with the Almighty God. So how does this work? Our Scripture reading today tells us how Jesus came and died for us, even though we were still sinners. It is because of Jesus' death that we have been made right in the sight of God. Now our friendship with God can be restored.

It doesn't end there. Our reading also tells us that because God loves us so dearly, He has given us the Holy Spirit to fill our hearts with His love (v5). We don't deserve any of this, but God wanted to reach out to us and provide a way for us to be His friends. Jesus the Son takes away our sins when we confess them and say sorry, the Father hears our prayers because of what Jesus has done and the Spirit guides us and helps us to live godly lives. God provides a friendship that helps us in everything we do. However, friendship with God can be like any other friendship. The more you talk and listen to what each other has to say, the deeper the relationship can go. When we don't talk and listen to God so much we can lose touch with Him. So stay connected and keep talking.

CHALLENGE

Try asking yourself a few questions to gauge where you are with God: how deep is my friendship with God? How much time do I spend getting to know God more and listening to Him? How can I deepen my friendship with God?

MON 18 JAN

READ:

JAMES 2:14–24

KEY VERSE v23

'"Abraham believed God, and it was credited to him as righteousness," and he was called God's friend.'

ABRAHAM HAD A strong faith in God and God alone. He had deep confidence in God and trusted Him utterly. Abraham was able to trust God like this because he knew God to be his great, good and faithful friend. He trusted God's words to him and chose to listen and follow what God said. Taking God at His word, Abraham stepped out from all that he knew and loved and followed God into a strange land with an uncertain destination. Later on, he was willing to surrender the most precious thing he had into God's hands. What faith! What friendship! What a challenge! If it came to it, could you trust God with everything you have?

We are told that God saw Abraham as godly and righteous, because of his faith. Perhaps, to us, Abraham is an extraordinary character with the kind of faith we could never emulate. Or maybe Abraham was just like you and me; a person who tried to hear God, do his best to follow Him and rely on Him to guide his path through life. We don't have to be extraordinary to be God's friend. We make a start by choosing to trust Him.

PRAY

Thank You, Father, that You are a true and trustworthy friend. Help me to put my confidence in You and to look to You for guidance in my life. Amen.

READ: LUKE 5:27–32

TUES 19 JAN

KEY VERSE V29

'Levi held a great banquet for Jesus ... and a large crowd of tax collectors and others were eating with them.'

IF YOU WERE going out for a meal, who would you take with you? Or, if you won a holiday abroad, who would be the best person to take? Would it be someone you didn't know very well or your best friend? Probably your friend! Most of us wouldn't choose people we know very little about or people who are seen as undesirable by others. In Jesus' time, tax collectors were despised. They were usually dishonest, untrustworthy, greedy and corrupt. Worst of all, they took money from their own people and gave it to the Romans, who had invaded the country. Tax collectors were traitors! Yet Jesus wanted to spend time with them.

Jesus chose outsiders, like tax collectors, because He wanted to bring the good news to those who really needed it, not the people who thought they already knew it all. Jesus wasn't afraid to be seen with those no one else wanted to be seen with! He put His own reputation at risk so that they might know God.

THINK

Think about this: who do you try to avoid? Who are the people you just don't get along with? Do they know God? Could you be the person who shares God's love with them?

WED 20 JAN

READ: ECCLESIASTES 4:7–12

KEY VERSE V9

'Two are better than one'

I HAVE TO admit that I am not a very good team player! I understand the value of teamwork and enjoy it when I get involved, but the truth is I prefer to do things on my own. Nevertheless, it's always good to have a friend around; someone you can talk to, laugh with and help out. I'm sure we can all remember times when having someone else with us would have made a real difference to a situation we were facing.

I used to teach Outdoor Pursuits, which involved a lot of teamwork. One activity involved using climbing equipment to get high into a tree and then descending using abseiling techniques. The golden rule was never to do this alone. It was a sunny day in May and I fancied some climbing. No one else was around, but I decided to climb the biggest oak tree anyway. It wasn't long before I became tangled in a climbing rope, some 90 feet in the air. If it wasn't for a work colleague making an impromptu appearance on his day off I could still be there now! That day I learned the hard way that two are definitely better than one.

CHALLENGE

If you don't already have someone to mentor you, try to find someone. This might be a youth leader or any older Christian you trust. It can make a big difference in your life and your faith!

READ: EPHESIANS 6:1–4

KEY VERSE V2

'"Honour your father and mother" – which is the first commandment with a promise'

I REMEMBER AS a child it was very difficult to 'honour' my father. He sometimes got it wrong. He didn't always listen when I tried to explain why and how things had happened: he would react first and I would try to get out of the way quick to avoid his outburst. So you can imagine my surprise when I first read our key verse today. I was about 18 years old, I'd not been a Christian very long and I found it very hard to take on board. After all, I was a man now and I was ready to stand up to my dad and get my own back.

It didn't work out this way, though. You see, God had changed me in many different ways, including my attitude. I began to find that I was able to sit down with my dad and work things out. My dad talked about how he saw me getting out of control and not being obedient and I talked about how I felt unloved as a son. Our conversations brought us closer than we'd ever been before.

God has commanded us to honour our parents. I know this can be hard but perhaps if I'd done this all along I could have had a friendship with my dad long before I reached 18.

PRAY

Ask God to help you when you struggle with doing as your parents ask. And if you are really struggling at home, talk to someone you trust. Ask God to bring peace in your home and friendship between you and your mum, dad or carer.

FRI 22 JAN

READ:
ROMANS 12:1–13

KEY VERSE v5

'in Christ we, though many, form one body, and each member belongs to all the others.'

THE CHURCH FAMILY is not much different to the family you live with. There are going to be times when personalities clash, things get heated and people argue. It would be great if the Church were perfect, but unfortunately that's not the case. The Church is made up of real people and people are imperfect.

Living with one another as the Body of Christ also includes loving one another. As our key verse says, we are many parts of one Body, and we all belong to each other. Belonging to each other and to the Body of Christ can be difficult, but when we love one another it is the best place to be. Within the Church family, we can use our gifts and see others using the gifts God has given them. We try to work in harmony with each other and to build friendships that enable us to grow into mature Christians. If I am not doing my part, the Church is worse off for this. The Body needs my gifts and my friendship. I need other people, too.

THINK

How meaningful are your friendships with people at church? How can you get to know them better? How can you serve them?

WEEKEND 23/24 JAN

READ:
JAMES 2:14–26

KEY VERSE
V14

'What good is it ... if someone claims to have faith but has no deeds?'

PT1 DISCIPLINE

WHAT BAD HABITS annoy you most? Maybe your dad has a really loud and embarrassing laugh or perhaps your sister leaves her dirty socks lying around the house. Do you have any habits that you know annoy other people? Have you perhaps tried to break your bad habit?

We all have habits. Some of them are good, some are bad, and some are just plain weird! Think about your routines in the morning or evening, either when getting up or going to bed. Do you have to do things in

CONTINUED▸▸

CONTINUED

a certain order? For example, I can't have breakfast until after I'm dressed. This is one habit I've got into. My mum has developed a habit in the way she hangs washing on the line – similar items must all be grouped together!

I often read about how long it takes to make something a habit. Although it must differ from person to person, many people seem to agree that if you do something repeatedly for three weeks, it starts, at least, to become a habit. We can think of developing habits as developing certain disciplines. We should be purposeful in thinking about which disciplines we want to develop. Having faith in Jesus is great and really important, but sooner or later this faith should affect our words and our actions. Over the next few days we'll be thinking about some of the ways in which our words and actions should change – disciplines we can develop to live in a wiser, more godly way.

PRAY

Lord God, as I think about spiritual disciplines, please show me which habits I should work on and develop. Help me to become more mature and to follow You more closely. Amen.

READ:
2 TIMOTHY 3:10–17

KEY VERSE V16

'All Scripture is God-breathed and is useful for teaching, rebuking, correcting and training in righteousness'

THE FIRST DISCIPLINE we're looking at is Bible study. The very fact you are reading this shows that you're probably prepared to develop this discipline!

Today's verse points out why this habit is important. The Bible is an important means of God's guidance for us. By studying it, we are allowing God to equip us to become better followers of Him and to fulfil the plans He has for us.

If you don't yet study the Bible every day, challenge yourself to set aside 15–20 minutes to do this and reflect on what you've read. How quickly does it start to become a habit? Think about the time of day when you do this. Are you always in a rush in the morning, struggling to fit it in? Do you find it difficult to stay awake and concentrate just before bed?

If you have already developed the discipline of studying God's Word at a regular point in the day, then think about how you could bring it in at other times as well. For example, maybe you could stick a Bible verse onto your mirror where you will see it often, or set one as a reminder on your phone. Try to make God's Word a more central part of your life.

CHALLENGE

Reflect again on what you've read today. What might be an appropriate challenge for you in the coming week?

TUES 26 JAN

READ: 1 THESSALONIANS 5:16–24

KEY VERSE v17

'pray continually'

ANOTHER KEY DISCIPLINE we need to focus on is prayer. There are many different reasons as to why prayer is important, and today's verse makes it clear that prayer is crucial and should be a central part of our daily life.

When something significant happens during the day, is your first thought to turn to God in prayer? It may be to ask for help or it may be to thank Him for something. Personally I know that so often I don't think to talk to God about something until later on in the day. My initial reaction is: how can I deal with the situation myself? Or: who can I ring or text about the situation?

As well as prayer being a feature throughout our day, we should also set aside specific time each day to devote to prayer. If you're anything like me then maybe your mind easily wanders during these prayer times. I've found that a prayer journal really can help. It helps to focus your thoughts and enables you to look back and see ways in which your prayers have been answered.

CHALLENGE

Do you pray every day? How often and for how long? Do you give time to listen for a response from God or do you quickly rush on to the next thing after praying? Could you think about starting a prayer journal to help?

READ: HEBREWS 10:19–25

KEY VERSE v25

'not giving up meeting together, as some are in the habit of doing, but encouraging one another'

IN TODAY'S WORLD, we often have many different opportunities open to us and so our lives can be very busy. With school or college work, sports clubs, socialising with friends, part-time jobs etc, it's a wonder that we're able to fit in any involvement with our local church and/or youth group. Attending church and meeting with other Christians can easily slip down our list of priorities. But today's reading reminds us that meeting with other Christians is another important discipline to develop.

When we meet with other Christians, we should be in the habit of encouraging one another and spurring each other on in our faith. Think about who you generally turn to for advice when you need help in making a decision. Do they usually give godly advice? Think too about what happens when people come to you for advice. Do you tell them what you think they want to hear, or do you really think and pray about the advice you give? Proverbs 27:17 tells us that, as friends, we can be instrumental in developing each other. Do you take that seriously in your own relationships?

THINK

Do you allow other Christians to influence your life by meeting with them regularly? What relationships might God be encouraging you to invest more time in?

THURS 28 JAN

READ:
COLOSSIANS 3:16–25

KEY VERSE v23

'Whatever you do, work at it with all your heart, as working for the Lord, not for human masters'

YESTERDAY WE THOUGHT about how being involved in our local church and spending time with other Christians are important habits to develop. The way in which we serve and give our time and skills for others is another important spiritual discipline. You may already be heavily involved in your church, maybe helping with the children's work, serving tea and coffee, or playing in the worship band. Today's verse tells us that everything we do (not just volunteering at church) should be done as if we are doing it for God.

Perhaps helping at church on a Sunday is already a priority for you. But how do you think about serving God at other times in the week? Are there other opportunities during the week when you could use your time to serve God? Could you offer to babysit so that someone can attend an event at church? Or could you perhaps visit a member of the church who is elderly or unwell?

Even if you don't currently have extra time to spare during the week, think about what does actually occupy your time. Today's Bible verse reminds us that even when we're not obviously serving God in what we're doing, we should do whatever we do as if it were for God.

PRAY

Father, thank You for giving me skills and talents. Please show me how You want me to use these skills, then give me opportunities to do those things. Amen.

READ: 1 CHRONICLES 16:23–36

KEY VERSE v29

'Worship the LORD in the splendour of his holiness.'

THE NEXT SPIRITUAL discipline we are going to look at is worship. Worship features throughout the Bible. In Genesis we read of how Cain and Abel made offerings to God (Gen. 4:3–5). We can read and enjoy David's songs of worship in the book of Psalms, and also read about him dancing before the Lord (2 Sam. 6:14). We can even find amazing descriptions of worship in Revelation (eg Rev. 19:1–8). And right throughout the Bible there are numerous other examples of people worshipping God.

To worship means to acknowledge how great God is, in both our words and our actions. Worship should not be all about us but should focus on God. Taking part in worship reminds us of who God is and who we are; people created and loved by God.

Because of the wide variety of kinds of worship in the Bible, we should be reminded that there is no one right way to do it. Worship is not just about singing songs at church on a Sunday. Our whole lives should be acts of worship (Rom. 12:1), pointing to God and who He is.

THINK

Reflect on your own experiences of worship. Is it a regular part of your life, and not just on a Sunday?

WEEKEND
30/31 JAN

READ:
1 CORINTHIANS 9:24–27

KEY VERSE v25

'Everyone who competes in the games goes into strict training.'

OVER THE WEEKEND we will take a quick break from looking at individual disciplines we should be trying to develop and think more generally about why being disciplined is important.

Some people seem to be remarkably self-disciplined. They manage to complete all their homework on the night they get it, and never leave deadlines hanging over them until the last minute. Unfortunately I'm not organised enough to be like that!

Paul gives us real food for thought in today's reading. We should be disciplined in training ourselves to do what God wants us to do. If we profess to be Christians and follow Christ, then we must practise what we preach.

Many people are put off Christianity because they see the hypocrisy with which so many so-called 'Christians' live their lives. On the one hand, these 'Christians' talk about a message of peace and forgiveness, but then they gossip nastily about other people. Or, perhaps, they believe that everybody should attend all the church services and youth events on offer, but then they go out and get drunk every Friday night.

Paul likens this kind of behaviour to the risk of being disqualified. What good is it to say that people should live a Christian lifestyle, if we are not seen to make the effort ourselves? When we are seen to live up to the claims we make, then people will respect us and be more interested in what we have to say.

CHALLENGE

Do you need to develop more self-discipline and train yourself further in any aspects of your life? Ask God to coach you in your training.

MON 1 FEB

READ:

ACTS 1:1–11

KEY VERSE V8

'you will be my witnesses ... to the ends of the earth.'

WE'RE BACK AGAIN to looking at some of the spiritual disciplines we should be developing. Next up, evangelism. The concept of sharing our faith often scares us. But if we truly believe the good news of the gospel, if we catch a glimpse of Jesus and see how amazing He is, surely we will be inspired to share this with other people.

Notice how today's key verse uses the word 'will'. Evangelism is a command – a compulsion, not an option. Of course, it's as we're filled with the Holy Spirit that evangelism becomes easier and more natural. But, even so, we must choose to take opportunities to share our faith when those opportunities arrive.

Sometimes people go through life wanting the benefits of the Christian life without the challenges. They want a God who loves them and cares about them, but don't want to have to talk about that with somebody else! But the Bible is clear: we need to share our faith with others.

THINK

Most people who become Christians hear the good news through a relationship with a friend. Do you pray for your friends, asking God that they would come to know Him? Do you look for opportunities to talk to them about God?

READ: 1 CORINTHIANS 16:1–4

TUES 2 FEB

KEY VERSE V2

'each one of you should set aside a sum of money in keeping with your income'

TODAY'S SPIRITUAL DISCIPLINE is about how we use our money. Throughout the Bible there are a lot of references to money: how we are to use it and how we are to give some to the work of God. As a young person, it can be easy to think that this doesn't really apply to us. However, as we think about the need to form positive habits, it makes sense to start while we are young.

The Bible frequently warns of the dangers of becoming too attached to money and riches. Luke 12:34 says, 'For where your treasure is, there your heart will be also.' If we are prepared to give money for God's purposes, then it communicates that He's a priority for us.

Proverbs 3:5 tells us to 'Trust in the LORD with all your heart and lean not on your own understanding'. Are we prepared to put our trust in God's ability to provide for us? Do we perhaps think we'll be better off if we can buy a certain new gadget or the latest fashion accessory? Or do we sacrifice our money to God, trusting that He will look after our every need?

PRAY

Thank You, God, that You were willing to sacrifice Your Son for me. Help me to be prepared to give up things for You. In particular, help me to establish the good habit of giving money to You and Your work. Amen.

READ: MATTHEW 6:16–18

KEY VERSE v16

'When you fast'

THE LAST SPIRITUAL discipline we'll look at is fasting. Many of us may find fasting the spiritual discipline we struggle with the most. It's certainly the case for me. As with evangelism, however, fasting is not to be seen as optional. Our reading talks about *when* you fast, not *if* you fast.

So why do it? Going without a meal gives us extra time to spend with God and when we feel hungry it reminds us to turn to God in prayer instead. It also helps us to depend on God, relying on Him for strength when we find things difficult. Focusing on God rather than food can help us gain a clearer spiritual perspective on life.

But how do we go about it? If you've never fasted before, it's best to start small, perhaps just missing one meal, but drinking water. Don't choose a day when you'll need to be very active and stop if you're feeling dizzy or faint.

If your parents feel strongly that you should not fast, respect their views. If you're ill, or have diabetes, or if you sometimes struggle with eating in general, you can fast from other things instead. For example, why not go without TV, caffeine, meat or social networking sites?

CHALLENGE

Have you ever fasted? Why or why not? How could you develop this as one of your spiritual disciplines?

READ: ECCLESIASTES 8:9–17

KEY VERSE V15

'So I commend the enjoyment of life, because there is nothing better for a person'

OFTEN WE THINK of disciplined people as boring, never able to have fun or be spontaneous. Many people believe that the Christian life has to be like that. But that's just not the case! In today's verse we are told that it is good to enjoy life and have fun.

Being a self-disciplined Christian means that we can go and have fun, as long as we remain in control of our actions and words. One of my friends at university had a group of friends who regularly went out drinking. He struggled, as a Christian, to know what he should do in this situation. On the one hand, he could refuse to go out with them, risking coming across as dull and boring. On the other hand, he could go out and join in their excessive drinking and drunken behaviour. In the end, he decided that he wanted to show that you could be a Christian and have a good time, without getting drunk. When he went out with them he limited himself to two alcoholic drinks a night. His friends came to really respect his strict two drinks only policy, and many went on to ask him about his Christian faith.

THINK

How do you relate to those around you who aren't Christians? Are you able to show self-discipline in the way you conduct yourself? How might God want you to alter the way you act around others?

FRI 5 FEB

READ: DEUTERONOMY 6:20–25

KEY VERSE V24

'The LORD commanded us to obey all these decrees ... so that we might always prosper'

DEVELOPING SPIRITUAL DISCIPLINES is rather like an athlete training for an event. Athletes think about all aspects of their lifestyle. As well as physical exercise, they take care to eat the right food, and they avoid drugs and alcohol. In training ourselves to be godly, we need to think about all aspects of our lives. It is no use focusing on just one of the spiritual disciplines. All have a significant part to play in developing godliness.

We may think that we are doing pretty well with our spiritual disciplines, but I've been challenged by the way that athletes do not get complacent and stop working hard. They may be the best and always come first, but they strive to be even better. There's always something more that could be achieved; another record that could be broken.

Today's reading reminds us that we don't follow God's commands and develop spiritual disciplines just to feel good about ourselves. No, the reward is much greater than that. If we follow God's commands, we open ourselves up to receive all kinds of blessings. What an incentive. Better than any Olympic gold medal!

PRAY

Lord, please show me the ways in which You would like me to develop. Give me the strength and the self-discipline to become more of the person You want me to be. Amen.

READ:
EPHESIANS 4:7–13

KEY VERSE
V8

'[Christ] gave gifts to his people.'

PT1 TALENT

CONGRATULATIONS! YOU'RE TALENTED! Maybe you already know that. Maybe you have a good idea what your talents are and they're very obvious to everyone around you too. Or maybe you find it difficult to believe that you have any talents at all. Maybe you've been given the message that you're stupid or useless so often that you've taken that message to heart.

CONTINUED»

CONTINUED»

Whatever we believe about how talented we are, the Bible tells us clearly that God has given each of us a special 'gift'. Paul, who wrote these words, is probably talking about God's grace and forgiveness more than anything else. But as we read on, we find that one of the effects of God's grace in our lives is that God gives each of us unique skills and talents.

So if you struggle to believe you have any kind of talent at all, take Paul's words to heart. God's grace – and the talents that grace brings – is for each one of us, including you.

On the other hand, if you already know you're talented, that's great. But don't think too highly of yourself because of that. Everyone else is talented too! Our talents shouldn't make us proud of ourselves. They should inspire us to worship the God who gave us our talents and enable us to play a part in strengthening the Church (v12).

In this series of readings, we'll investigate what talent looks like and how to use our talents and make the most of them. We'll go on to think about how we can spot talents in other people and encourage them in those talents, too.

THINK

What talents do you think you have? If you're not sure, ask someone who knows you well. Pray and ask God to show you more clearly what talents He has given you and how you should use them.

READ: JEREMIAH 1:4–10

KEY VERSE V5

'Before I formed you in the womb I knew you'

IT NEVER CEASES to amaze me that God lets me do the things I enjoy. I love writing and I love telling people about Jesus. I'd probably do them even if they weren't my job. But for some reason, I'm employed to do both. God has created each of us differently. He made us each unique, with unique passions. God has given us these passions, not only to enjoy, but to glorify Him, and if we hand our passions over to Him they can reach their fullest potential.

Sometimes the way to discover our talents is to ask ourselves what motivates us, to ask what we're passionate about. That's not to say that everything we enjoy will be used by God. (My love of jelly beans is yet to lead to any kind of employment or to bring anyone to Jesus.) But God knows us better than we know ourselves, and so we can trust Him to use what we're passionate about for His purposes. As the key verse says, God's known us since the beginning. He knows us better than we know ourselves. God's purposes are perfect and He has made us all to do amazing but different things. If you want to discover God's purposes for you, why not start by asking what it is that gets you up in the morning?

PRAY

Ask God to show you what your passions are, and from there to show you the talents He's given you. The answers to these questions may already be obvious!

TUES 9 FEB

READ:
EXODUS 31:1–11

KEY VERSE V6

'I have given ability to all the skilled workers to make everything I have commanded you'

THERE'S SOMETHING VERY special about a masterpiece. A truly exceptional piece of art will take your breath away when you see it. The same is true of an outstanding piece of music or a beautifully designed building. Perhaps masterpieces affect us so powerfully because God inspired the people who created these things and gave them the talents they needed to create them.

God doesn't just give us talents that we can use in church on Sunday. Yes, He does give some people gifts of teaching, evangelism and prophecy, as we saw at the weekend (Eph. 4:11), but the gifts God gives are far wider and more diverse than that. For example, in this reading from Exodus, God gives certain people skills in art, craft and metalwork. He gives us all kinds of different skills today too. Whether we're clever, sporty, arty or good at looking after other people, these talents come from God. The challenge for us is the same as for Bezalel and Oholiab; to use our talents to serve God.

THINK

Think about the talents God has given you. Are you using them for your own ambitions or have you devoted them to God? Commit to using those talents to serve Him. Ask for His help in doing that.

READ: 1 CORINTHIANS 12:1–11

KEY VERSE V1

'Now about the gifts of the Spirit, brothers and sisters, I do not want you to be uninformed.'

HAS SOMEONE EVER given you a message from God? Someone I'd only met once was preaching at my church. During the service, this guy singled me out and gave me an incredibly encouraging message. God had told him all about some challenges I was facing at the time – there's absolutely no other way he could have known – and he explained to me how God was going to carry me through these challenges.

This is an example of a 'message of knowledge' (v8). This gift and the others mentioned in 1 Corinthians 12 are like talents, but a little different. Spiritual gifts are given to anyone (v11), just like talents, but unlike talents, we don't automatically have spiritual gifts. While God gives everyone talents, He reserves spiritual gifts for people who know Him and want to follow Him. So Christians can have both! Spiritual gifts are abilities which are only possible by the power of God. When someone uses a spiritual gift, it can be very impressive, but, just like talents, spiritual gifts aren't for our own benefit; they're to enable us to help other people. God wants to give you spiritual gifts too. Let Him fill you with the Holy Spirit and see what happens next!

PRAY

Ask God to fill you with the Holy Spirit. Ask Him to make you more like Jesus and to show you what spiritual gifts He has given you or wants to give you.

THURS 11 FEB

READ:
ROMANS 12:3–8

KEY VERSE v7

'if it is serving, then serve;
if it is teaching, then teach'

I HAVE A vase in my cupboard that I don't particularly like. A friend gave it to me as a present once, and I only bring it out when I know this friend is coming to visit. The rest of the time, the vase sits in the cupboard, collecting dust. If the vase was more pleasant to look at, I'd keep it on the windowsill all the time, not just to avoid upsetting my friend, but so that everyone who saw the vase could appreciate it too.

The gifts God gives us are much more pleasing and valuable than the vase in my cupboard! So we should make use of whatever talents we have, out of respect for other people (vv4–5) and out of a desire to honour God (v6). In Matthew 25:14–30, Jesus tells a parable which reinforces this idea. Read it now!

This parable doesn't mean that if we don't use our talents, God will leave us in pain and torment forever. That's not the truth of the gospel. But the parable does tell us clearly that how we live now matters. God has blessed us in so many ways and it's our duty to use what God has given us. When we use our talents, we honour God, we help the people around us and we give them a glimpse of the God who enabled us to do what we're doing.

CHALLENGE

Use your talents! Think of one particular talent or skill you have. Find a way to use it regularly, so that other people can catch a glimpse of God.

READ: JAMES 1:12–18

KEY VERSE v17

'Every good and perfect gift is from above, coming down from the Father'

WHAT'S THE BEST present anyone's ever given you? How did you react to this present? I'm guessing it made you very happy, that you wanted to make use of this present straightaway and that you were extremely grateful to the person who gave it to you. Did it make you proud of yourself? Of course not. What a strange thing to ask. But I bet you can think of someone who's proud of themselves because of the talents they have.

This is just as bizarre as being proud of yourself because of a present you were given or because of your height or your hair colour. We have no control over the talents we have, so being proud of our talents is ridiculous! Our talents, like every other good thing in our lives, are gifts from God. Our response to our talents should be to use them, as we've already said. But before we even do that, we should respond by acknowledging that our talents are gifts from God and by thanking Him for what He has given us.

THINK

Do you ever take your talents for granted? Do you ever fall into the trap of being proud of your talents? Decide now to be thankful to God for what He has given you.

WEEKEND

13/14 FEB

READ:
COLOSSIANS 3:12–17

KEY VERSE v17

'And whatever you do, whether in word or deed, do it all in the name of the Lord Jesus'

I WATCH A lot of football – perhaps an antisocial amount – and one thing that always amuses me is the celebrations. For some reason, the individual who has the final say in scoring seems to take all the credit, to run around pointing at himself, grabbing all the glory, ignoring his teammates. No matter how much his team may have done to create the opportunity for him, the selfish scorer would rather claim all the credit for himself.

Often, when we're good at something, it goes to our heads. We can be tempted to ignore that it was God who gave us the talent. This might even be something that you don't think of as 'spiritual'.

When you're complimented on something, do you give the glory to Jesus, or just enjoy the limelight? This can happen in churches as well: when someone compliments something we've done, be it a talk or leading worship, all that glory has to be reflected back to God, the one who gave us the talent.

There are two challenges here. First, acknowledging God in all you do. This is the 'whatever you do' part of the verse. Don't pack the 'God stuff' into one corner of your life, but remember that He created ALL of you, and has given you talents that you can use outside of the church walls. Second, we are called to acknowledge God at all times, rather than letting people think that our talents point to how wonderful we are. All those gifts and talents come from God, so it only seems fair to let them point back to Him!

PRAY

Dear God, thank You so much for the talents You've given me. Please give me opportunities to glorify Your name through these. Amen.

MON 15 FEB

READ:
1 SAMUEL 17:12–24,32–51

KEY VERSE v45

'You come against me with sword and spear and javelin, but I come against you in the name of the LORD Almighty'

PERHAPS THE MOST famous story about King David is his defeat of Goliath. One swing of a slingshot and – BAM – the most fearsome foe Israel were facing was defeated. A lucky shot, a precise calculation of wind speed and trigonometry, or something bigger?

What's interesting about David's moment is that it comes straight after David is anointed by Samuel (see 1 Sam. 16:1–13). There seems to be a direct relationship between God empowering someone, and that person's talents being noticed and used. And perhaps that is the point. David approached the battlefield knowing that all he had to offer came from God, knowing that from the world's perspective there was nothing particular about himself that would lead him to victory.

In the midst of an amazing victory, David points to the One who made it happen, rather than himself. No wonder he is remembered as such a good king. It is God who gives us our talents, and when we're humble enough to acknowledge that, these talents can be used to their full potential.

CHALLENGE

Are you humble enough with what God has given you? Find opportunities to humble yourself when things seem to be going well.

READ:
MATTHEW 25:14–30

KEY VERSE v21

'Well done, good and faithful servant!
You have been faithful with a few things;
I will put you in charge of many things.'

I LOVE COMIC books, probably more than an adult should. Perhaps the moment from any comic that has become the biggest part of our culture is the challenge of Peter Parker's Spider-Man: 'With great power comes great responsibility.' As well as inspiring Spider-Man's quest, it also neatly sums up this passage. When the master returns from his journey, each servant's performance is measured in relation to what was given to him, rather than the other servants.

The challenge here is not about achieving great things, it's about using what God has given us to the full. When I turned 21, I began to realise I'd never be an Oscar-winning actor. So there's no point in me aiming to do that! I'm just about getting to the point where I understand what God has made me good at, and it's my job to make the most of that. God has different plans for each of us, and it's what we do with the gifts we've been given to use that matters. So stop comparing your talents to those around you. God has made you unique, with a set of talents and a plan individual to you.

THINK

Do you spend too much time wishing you had other people's talents? The funny thing is there's probably someone out there who wishes they had yours! So ask yourself: am I doing enough with what God has given *me*?

WED 17 FEB

READ: 1 KINGS 19:19–21

KEY VERSE v19

'Elijah went from there and found Elisha ... Elijah went up to him and threw his cloak around him.'

DO YOU HAVE a Yoda? Just in case you've never seen *Star Wars*, I should explain that Yoda is a Jedi Master who helps Luke Skywalker hone his own Jedi skills. Yoda doesn't look very impressive to start with, but he turns out to be immensely wise and skilful. He helps Luke to become far stronger than he could have been on his own.

Elijah does something similar for Elisha. He notices the calling and abilities God has given Elisha, takes him under his wing, teaches him to do what he himself is doing and develops the talents God has given him. Because of this, when Elijah is finally taken into heaven, Elisha is ready to carry on Elijah's work. Elisha's experience of being mentored helps him to make the most of his God-given abilities.

My Yoda is called Jonny. I love writing, helping people understand the Bible and coming up with new ideas for both of these things. I asked Jonny to mentor me because he's brilliant at this. I want to get as good as he is at this stuff. I meet Jonny for coffee every now and then. He'll ask me awkward questions and challenge a few of my assumptions, but mostly encourage me in what I'm doing. Who could do that for you?

CHALLENGE

Find a mentor. Find someone with similar talents to you, who could encourage you and help you develop your skills. Then take the plunge and ask for help.

READ:
PROVERBS 10:1–9

KEY VERSE V4

'Lazy hands make for poverty, but diligent hands bring wealth.'

IT'S NOT OFTEN that I'll quote a horror writer, but in this case, I think Stephen King is on to something. He once had this to say about talent: 'Talent is cheaper than table salt. What separates the talented individual from the successful one is a lot of hard work.' Proverbs puts the same truth in an even punchier way: lazy people are soon poor; hard workers get rich.

Hard work might not always make us rich and successful in worldly terms, but whatever we want to achieve, hard work is vital. It's not enough just to be talented. If we want to make any kind of difference to our own situation, to the people around us or in extending God's kingdom, we must be prepared to put in the work.

Take musicians for example. Often they seem to be born with an innate passion and talent for music. But if they never pick up an instrument, have lessons and practice daily, their talent would come to nothing – what a waste that would be! Take a moment to think about your own talent. Do you invest the time, effort and energy that will allow it to flourish? To play our part in bringing God's kingdom on earth, we need to be disciplined, committed and persevering.

PRAY

Lord God, thank You for the talents You have given me. Please help me to be disciplined, committed and persevering, so that I can play a part in bringing Your kingdom on earth. Amen.

FRI 19 FEB

READ:
EXODUS 3:1–12

KEY VERSES VV11–12

'But Moses said to God, "Who am I that I should go ...?" And God said, "I will be with you."'

MOSES IS RENOWNED as a great hero of the Christian and Jewish faiths. But before he did any of the great things he is known for, Moses was scared, timid and full of self-doubt. This is the Moses we meet in Exodus 3. God's response to Moses' self-doubt is fascinating. Moses asks, 'Who am I?' God replies, 'I will be with you.' God doesn't actually answer the question! Perhaps God wanted Moses to understand that it didn't matter how important or powerful he was in his own right. God Himself would be with Moses and His power and authority would make Moses powerful and authoritative. God also deals with Moses' worries about his lack of skill as a speaker (see Exod. 4:11–12).

If we feel scared, timid and full of self-doubt, there's encouragement for us here. None of us are anything special in ourselves, but our God is with us. He will equip us for every task He calls us to. If we feel confident and self-assured, we need to be careful. If Moses had tried to confront Pharaoh and lead the Israelites relying on his own abilities, he would have got into a mess. We face the same pitfall today. Whatever we do, however confident and talented we feel, let's rely on God to help us and strengthen us.

CHALLENGE

What challenges are you facing today? Rely on God to be with you to guide you and give you wisdom and skill.

WEEKEND 20/21 FEB

READ:
GENESIS 1:26–28

KEY VERSE
V26

'Then God said, "Let us make mankind in our image, in our likeness"'

THE TRINITY PT2

WELCOME BACK TO our notes on the Trinity! So far we've looked at how the Trinity shows us that God is a God of relationship. In this second section we're going to focus on how the Trinity helps us, whether that's by revealing things to us, helping us rest or empowering us to do great things for God.

Today we start with a very important fact. God created us in His image. Genesis tells us that God created the animals, plants and trees, but He created *us* in His

CONTINUED»

CONTINUED

own image. Each Person of God spoke to the other and decided to make human beings like themselves.

Humans are unique because we're in touch with our mind, body, emotions and spirit – and we have free choice. After a lot of exercise we are physically tired, but mentally we're really stimulated because, so scientists tell us, of all those endorphins whizzing around our bodies. However, after a long exam we can be mentally exhausted yet physically charged with the energy to run it all off. After receiving bad news, our bodies may be fine but we can feel really down emotionally. You don't see monkeys having to deal with all of this!

Our makeup reflects, in measure, the makeup of the Trinity. We were given a body to use, a brain with which to make decisions, imagine and design, and a spirit – which the Holy Trinity breathed into us with 'the breath of life' (Gen. 2:7). So whatever we lack, whatever we need, God knows because He understands us as easily as He knows Himself! Wow!

PRAY

Lord, thank You that You have created us in Your image. Thank You for all You've given us to serve You with – our mind, body, emotions and spirit. And thank You for knowing and understanding us completely. Amen.

READ:
COLOSSIANS 1:15–23

MON 22 FEB

KEY VERSE V15

'The Son is the image of the invisible God, the firstborn over all creation.'

HOW MANY TIMES have you heard people cooing over babies, saying things like: 'Oh, isn't he cute? He looks just like his dad.' Or, 'Hasn't he got his dad's eyes?'

Paul tells the Church in Colosse that Jesus is just like His Dad. If they want to know what God is like, they only need to look at Jesus. Jesus is more than a good man, a healer, a storyteller, a wise man, a prophet, a freedom fighter or a politician. Paul tells us that Jesus is the image of the invisible God.

It is important for us to understand that Jesus isn't similar to or just a bit like God. He is the *exact* image of God. He reflects God. Jesus is God, God is Jesus. So we can know and understand God better through reading accounts of Jesus in the Bible. And as we read yesterday, we are also made in the image of God, so we can understand ourselves better too! Jesus knows our human temptations and struggles first hand. And because He is God, He knows the best way to help us through anything.

PRAY

Thank You, Jesus, that You are not remote from us as humans, but You became one of us. You understand the struggles of being human, even though You are God the Son. When we know You more, Jesus, we know more of God. Amen.

TUES 23 FEB

READ:
JOHN 10:22–36

KEY VERSE V29

'My Father … has given them to me … no one can snatch them out of my Father's hand.'

JESUS COULDN'T HAVE been more clear and upfront with the crowd if He'd tried. 'The Father and I are one,' He told an angry mob, who then picked up stones to kill Him. This statement would have so angered the crowd – they would have heard it as blatant blasphemy, yet Jesus was stating a fact. He is a member of the Trinity. The crowd could believe it or not!

Jesus and the Father are one. Nothing that Jesus does is without the Father's say-so and the Spirit's guidance and direction. They work in perfect harmony together.

We also read today about Jesus' 'sheep'. The sheep are His followers – you and me! Jesus says we can know His voice and be directed by Him, but more, He says that *no one* can take us away from God. Isn't this an amazing and comforting word for today? Whenever we feel weak, anxious or confused, we can rest and feel secure in this promise.

THINK

When people around you mock God or question His existence, what is your usual response? Knowing that He is always with you, does that give you the courage to make a stand for Him in the future?

READ: TITUS 3:4–8

KEY VERSES vv4–5

'when the kindness and love of God our Saviour appeared, he saved us'

WHO IS THE kindest person you know? One of your teachers or leaders at church? Or maybe it's one of your friends, parents or grandparents, or even a well-known celebrity? In what ways are they kind to you or other people?

When Paul writes to Titus, he describes God as a kind God. Kindness is described in the dictionary as a friendly, generous, helpful, considerate and loving quality, act or behaviour. This definition can really help us to understand the different aspects of the Trinity.

The quality of kindness can be linked to the Father who, even from before the foundation of the world, had prepared a rescue plan to save humankind from sin. This act of kindness saw the God of the universe shrink down by the Spirit's power into a tiny embryo, being born as a helpless human baby into very humble circumstances.

We can have the same behaviour as Jesus through the Holy Spirit living in us, giving us the power to live as He lived, to be kind as He was kind.

CHALLENGE

Jesus is the perfect example of the kindness of God. Here's our challenge today: if someone were to ask our friends to describe us, would they use the word 'kind'?

THURS 25 FEB

READ:

ACTS 2:1–12

KEY VERSE V4

'All of them were filled with the Holy Spirit and began to speak in other tongues'

WE'RE GOING TO spend a few days now focusing on the Holy Spirit. Today we read about the very first outpouring of the Holy Spirit after Jesus returned to heaven.

What do you get if you cross 12 weak, powerless apostles with the Holy Spirit? The answer is the first and probably greatest evangelistic event ever seen!

Try to remember when you read this that the disciples had all seen Jesus crucified. They were stunned to see the risen Lord Jesus and then sad to see Him ascend to heaven. They hadn't understood that Jesus had to return to the Father in order to send the Spirit. Hiding away from the world, the disciples were waiting on God, not knowing what to expect.

Suddenly, God gives them all His Holy Spirit, enabling a rough bunch of Galilean men, including fishermen and a tax collector, to speak in 15 different languages or more. There's no mention of fear at this point. The scene drew an enormous crowd, including Parthians, Medes, Elamites, Egyptians, Romans, Cretans and Arabs, who marvelled at what was going on.

PRAY

Thank You, Lord, for the first outpouring of Your Holy Spirit that drew people of all different languages, cultures and social backgrounds to You. Please enable the Holy Spirit in me to draw people to You through the way I live my life. Amen.

READ: GENESIS 41:38–40

KEY VERSE V38

'Can we find anyone like this man, one in whom is the spirit of God?'

FINALLY, AFTER BEING sold to traders by jealous brothers, years of slavery, being wrongly accused by his master's wife, then left to rot in prison, Joseph is summoned into the Pharaoh's presence and asked to interpret a dream that has confused all the wise men of Egypt. Instead of promoting his own ability, Joseph responds: 'I cannot do it ... but God will give Pharaoh the answer he desires' (Gen. 41:16).

Before the Pentecost, which we read about yesterday, the Spirit of God was only given to individuals at key times. Yet during these times, He always brought glory and honour to His name. After the interpretation of his dreams, Pharaoh exclaims that Joseph is so obviously filled with the Spirit of God that he needs to be put in a position of huge responsibility.

The Spirit enabled Joseph to interpret dreams, David to write songs, Elijah to perform miracles, Samson to judge Israel and a shy, feeble Gideon to defeat the Midianites!

THINK

The same Spirit who helped Joseph interpret dreams, Moses to speak to Pharaoh and Jonah to prophesy over the city of Nineveh is living inside you now. The third member of the Holy Trinity lives inside you, 24 hours a day. Think about that!

WEEKEND

27/28 FEB

READ:
1 CORINTHIANS 2:1–16

KEY VERSE V10

'these are the things God has revealed to us by his Spirit.'

HAVE YOU EVER been told by a friend, 'You *must* see this film' or 'You *must* get this album'?

A lot of socialising is about sharing the latest gadgets, music, games and fashion. Your friends reveal their lives to you – the things they enjoy – and, in turn, you do the same. Why? Because these things deepen our relationships and connect us with each other – and we were created for relationship.

In today's passage we see that the Holy Spirit also reveals things to us. Some of the wisest, cleverest people in the world cannot understand the wisdom of God or the nature of our free salvation in Jesus. Yet a five-year-old can completely understand that Jesus loves them and has died for them. It is not a matter of intelligence, but rather a matter of the Spirit revealing this truth to us. We didn't work it out for ourselves.

God speaks through His Spirit into the lives of humankind. He reveals the truth about Jesus' death for our sins, His resurrection and His ascension. He softens the hardest hearts and opens the blindest eyes, all because He loves each one of us more than we could ever imagine. He reveals things to us for the same reason we share things with each other – He wants to be closer to us, and He wants us to feel closer to Him.

CHALLENGE

Have you been trying hard to convince your friends about the truth of Christianity, but without success? Maybe you should be praying that the Spirit will reveal the salvation of God to your friends through your conversations. Don't rely on your own powers of persuasion!

MON 29 FEB

READ:
1 CORINTHIANS 12:1–11

KEY VERSE V4

'There are different kinds of gifts, but the same Spirit distributes them.'

DO YOU LIKE to give your treasured possessions names? Have you named your car, bike, guitar or piano? We, as humans, seem to like to name certain objects or call things 'she' or 'he' – but why? They have no personality of themselves; they are purely objects to be used at our command or disposal.

In Corinthians we see that the Spirit of God is completely different. The Spirit is not just a power source that makes us feel happy. He is not just an invisible thing that gives us certain gifts or talents. He is not a nameless entity. His name is the Holy Spirit, and the Holy Spirit has His own identity.

Paul is careful to point out that there is only one Holy Spirit, not many spirits of God. There is only one Spirit who gives to people all the gifts at His discretion. Paul refers to the Spirit as He, not because the Spirit looks or feels like a He, but because the Spirit of God is an entity; another equal member of the Trinity. Paul also tells us that the Spirit has intelligence, with a mind and will, and that He gives gifts to whomever He chooses.

THINK

When you pray to God, do you often speak to the Holy Spirit? If not, try to get to know Him better through talking to Him and reading about Him.

TUES 1 MAR

READ: 1 CORINTHIANS 12:7–27

KEY VERSE V7

'Now to each one the manifestation of the Spirit is given for the common good.'

A FEW SUMMERS ago I spent a week in Kosovo working with a mission that runs holiday Bible clubs. Our team of 17 very different people (aged 5 to 75) included English, South Americans, Australians, and Kosovans, all working together as one.

In explaining the gifts of the Spirit, Paul uses the analogy of a body. Each part has equal importance, yet looks very different and operates in a unique way. The eye, foot and head are obviously all very different, yet they are all vital if the body is to function properly.

The Holy Spirit gives gifts as He sees necessary: the gift of being wise, the gift of strong faith and, to some, the gift of healing others. The list goes on, but the reason for the gifts is not just to encourage and help the individual receiver to grow in Christ. Paul explains the bigger picture: the gifts of the Holy Spirit are given to the Body of Christ (that is, the Church) for its encouragement and growth.

Just like during my visit to Kosovo, the Spirit is working in the lives of believers to build up an international Church – that is Jesus' hands and feet on the earth.

PRAY

Pray about the gifts that will encourage your youth group or church to grow. A gift used behind the scenes will encourage God's work to grow just as much as a visible, public gift. Which gifts has God given you?

WED 2 MAR

READ:
GALATIANS 5:13–25

KEY VERSES VV22–23

'But the fruit of the Spirit is love, joy, peace, forbearance, kindness, goodness, faithfulness, gentleness and self-control.'

A FEW YEARS ago we bought some fruit trees and planted them in our garden. The following spring, we had a bet as to which one was the pear tree and which was the apple. My wife won the bet when our tiny tree produced an apple within a week.

Yesterday we looked at the gifts of the Spirit given to different people to build up the Church – the Body of Christ. The fruit of the Spirit is a little different to His gifts. It is seen in our character rather than in what we do for others. Like my tiny apple tree that produced a full-sized apple, we produce fruit if we put our roots into God and His Word.

In turn, our fruit gives glory back to the Father through the work of the Son, because people begin to make the connection between the way we live our lives and who we believe in (Jesus), learning then about who sent Him to die for us (the Father and the Spirit).

As the Spirit lives in us, He encourages us to give up our old lives and live a new, fruitful life of love, joy, peace, patience, kindness, goodness, faithfulness, gentleness and self-control.

CHALLENGE

Which fruit of the Spirit do you need more in your life at the moment? Ask the Holy Spirit to fill you and help you, and see how you get on over the next few days!

READ: JOHN 7:30–39

KEY VERSE v37

'Let anyone who is thirsty come to me and drink.'

HAVE YOU EVER been more than just merely thirsty – absolutely parched? There's nothing that can beat it when you eventually get that drink – especially if it's ice-cold, fresh water.

As He stands before the Pharisees, Jesus offers a drink to anyone who is thirsty – not physically but spiritually thirsty. Jesus says to the crowd that He is the source of this spiritual drink which anyone can receive.

The only way for someone to receive this spiritual drink (which is the Holy Spirit) is by coming to belief in the Son. The Father will then give the believer the Spirit through the Son, Jesus – an example of the Trinity at work in our Christian life. In today's reading, Jesus is offering the Holy Spirit to anyone (not just to prophets, kings and holy people) who will simply ask Him and believe in Him.

We can become thirsty as Christians if we let our relationship with God slip. We can feel dry, uninspired, unmotivated and unmoved. When we find ourselves feeling this way, let's go to the source who can fill us afresh today with 'rivers of living water'!

CHALLENGE

Are there people in your school or college who are spiritually thirsty? Do they know what they need to do to quench their spiritual thirst? Who will tell them if you won't?

FRI 4 MAR

READ:

HEBREWS 10:1–18

KEY VERSE v12

'when [Jesus] had offered for all time one sacrifice for sins, he sat down at the right hand of God'

HAVE YOU EVER worked really hard on a job, or on homework or revision, to then end the day with some relaxing down time? It feels good to sit down after completing a hard day's work – it's satisfying, isn't it?

Well, this is the sort of feeling behind the Old Testament imagery used in today's reading. After His once and for all sacrifice, Jesus sits down at the right hand of the Father because, as He said on the cross, 'It is finished' (John 19:30). The Trinity had achieved the master plan of saving the human race from the power of sin. So Jesus returned to His rightful place with the Father in heaven, and the Spirit testifies to this truth by revealing it to all humankind through the inspired words of the Bible. Here again we see the Triune God working and resting in perfect harmony.

Every member of the Trinity is needed to ensure our salvation, redemption and invitation to follow God. We need belief in the Son's mission, belief in the Father who sent His only Son, and belief in the Spirit's Words revealed through the gospel message.

THINK

God knows the importance of rest – and of resting in the company of others. Think about this coming weekend and how you'll have time to rest and recharge for the next week. Could you set aside some time to spend resting with God?

WEEKEND 5/6 MAR

READ:
PROVERBS 12:25–26

KEY VERSE
V25

'Anxiety weighs down the heart, but a kind word cheers it up.'

FRiENDSHiP PT2

SOCIAL NETWORKING SITES have their pros and cons. Through Facebook I have enjoyed renewed friendships with people from my past. On the other hand, some of the people who have found me I never wanted to see or hear from again! This is mainly because they reminded me of the days when I didn't know God. They aren't bad people but they were tied in with a part of my life that I chose to leave behind.

CONTINUED»

CONTINUED»

For example, I used to be friends with someone we'll call Dave, who constantly looked down on life. He had nothing good to say about anything and seemed very unhappy even to be alive. There was honestly nothing I could do to cheer Dave up. I tried and so did others, but I wasn't strong enough to help and I needed a friend who was more positive and encouraging towards me. Recently, Dave took his own life. I know this wasn't my fault: Dave needed specialist help, far beyond what I could offer. However, it was an awful thing to happen and it reminds me very powerfully that although I have needs, so do others. I need to work hard to encourage my friends.

We all need encouragement and it's our friends we rely on for this. As friends we are called to carry burdens for others. But as there is only ever so much someone can take, we also need people who can support us when we are hurting. This way we support one another and the burden is never too heavy to carry.

PRAY

Father God, would You help me to be the kind of friend that You want me to be. Help me to be an encourager even when times are tough, and even when I am low. I know You won't give me more than I can bear, but help me to be an encouragement to my friends and family. Amen.

READ: 2 TIMOTHY 3:1–17

KEY VERSES VV2,4

'People will be lovers of themselves ... rather than lovers of God'

AT THE MOMENT, Facebook tells me that I have 679 friends. It makes me wonder though: how many of those people do I really know? Do I know what makes them all tick? Do I even know where they all live? Probably not! Probably only a handful of these 679 people are true friends.

A guy I know is quite happy to add anyone who asks to be his friend on Facebook. Perhaps we should be more careful than this. The danger here is that when we associate ourselves with a 'group' or a 'person' people can assume that we see life the same way. More to the point, if we choose to associate with someone without really knowing what kind of person they are, we can find that they influence us very negatively. Today's reading shows what Paul wrote to Timothy about this issue. Paul knew that a lot of the people around Timothy would influence him and his church very badly, so he warned Timothy to stay away from them. We could learn from this advice. Let's be cautious about who we allow to influence us. As Paul says in another of his letters, 'Bad company corrupts good character' (1 Cor. 15:33).

CHALLENGE

Look at your friendship group or groups at the moment. What does the company you keep say about you? Are your friends influencing you positively or negatively?

TUES 8 MAR

READ: 1 THESSALONIANS 5:12–22

KEY VERSE v15

'Make sure that nobody pays back wrong for wrong, but always strive to do what is good for each other'

HAVE YOU EVER heard the term 'a vicious circle'? I find it frustrating when I see things happening like this: like a merry-go-round that just will not stop! For example, I have a disagreement with a friend and it turns into a serious argument. The argument causes a rift between us and makes it even less likely that one of us will back down. Then we disagree about whose fault it all was and what we should do about it, and the vicious circle continues. The argument just goes around and around with no sign of any solution.

When we have disagreements with our friends, we can break the vicious circle. We can be the solution to the problem! In today's reading, Paul gives us some valuable advice for healthy friendships and healthy churches. In particular, it's important to offer love and compassion, not to pay back wrong for wrong, even when we feel a friend has really wronged us. It only takes one person to make peace and an argument can be resolved. The Bible tells us that 'Blessed are the peacemakers, for they will be called children of God' (Matt. 5:9). Go be a peacemaker and change the world.

THINK

Just imagine what could happen if you were to back down from an argument. It's not always important to be right all the time. Backing down does not make you wrong but does create peace.

READ: JOB 19:13–19

WED 9 MAR

KEY VERSE v19

'All my intimate friends detest me; those I love have turned against me.'

HAS A FRIEND ever turned their back on you? One day they were your friend and then the next they seemed to have turned against you? You might never understand why this happened. Was it something I said? Was it something I did or didn't do? How can I make it better? Job asks some of these questions of his friends. When everything around him is falling apart he hopes his friends will support him, but they don't.

When this happens, it's hard to keep things in perspective. When a friend hurts us, we may want to hurt them back. When they spread rumours, we may want to retaliate. This isn't the best way to respond. Job calls out to God and tells Him all his worries. He complains to God and grieves over his situation. God can take all our emotions on the chin and still love us. Our God is big enough to know what are valid points and what is just moaning. God offers us a relationship in which we can be honest about everything and still be able to call Him our Friend.

CHALLENGE

When friends turn their back on you, take the problem to God and choose not to retaliate. You never know, by being a person of integrity, they may see that your friendship was well worth having.

THURS 10 MAR

READ:

PSALM 55:1–23

KEY VERSES VV12–13

'If an enemy were insulting me, I could endure it ... But it is you, a man like myself'

IT'S NOT EASY handling our emotions when friends turn on us. It can be hard to keep our words reasonable and our thoughts pure. After all, we are only human and when humans get hurt, they tend to try to protect themselves. Unfortunately, this can land us in hot water! Our human nature sometimes makes us want to hurt people back, to make them suffer, to spread rumours about them or to share their secrets with others. When we are hurt, we can think that hurting the person responsible will make us feel better.

But this is not the way that God wants us to live. Yes, people will hurt us at many points in our lives. Yes, even friends may turn on us and that can be very painful, but God never lets us down and never lets us go. When we hurt, God hurts with us. David was hurting. His closest friend was now the one who taunted him. His world was turning upside down. So, what did he do? He turned to God. 'As for me, I call to God, and the LORD saves me' (v16). No matter what happens in our friendships, God is with us and is waiting for us to call on Him.

THINK

How do you handle being taunted by people who were once your friends? Do you react in a negative way or do you take it to God?

READ: PROVERBS 26:17–28

KEY VERSE v28

'A lying tongue hates those it hurts, and a flattering mouth works ruin.'

AT TIMES, WE may discover that people who called themselves our friends turn out to be false friends. When this happens, the pain can be very deep. We may have trusted them deeply, told them things we haven't told others and been generous with our money, our time and our possessions. There is no easy fix when someone turns out to be a false friend. Usually only time and God's comfort heal the wounds. But, unfortunately, false friends do exist. So, how can you spot them?

When someone's actions don't add up to what they say – when they flatter you, compliment you and then do something that hurts you – beware. No amount of flowery words can cover up constant bad behaviour towards you. If this keeps happening then it might be time to walk away. One person I had to walk away from could sweet talk her way out of anything. I got into trouble for all the bad things she did because she had a way with words that I didn't. She even pointed the blame at me then pretended that there was nothing wrong. It took some time before I was brave enough to see that this was not a true friend.

PRAY

Lord God, give me wisdom to tell good friends from false friends. Help me to support and encourage the friends that I have; to really value them and not hurt them. Amen.

WEEKEND

12/13 MAR

READ:

COLOSSIANS 4:2–6

KEY VERSE V6

'Let your conversation be always full of grace, seasoned with salt, so that you may know how to answer everyone.'

THERE HAVE BEEN times in my life when I have messed up badly. For example, there was one occasion when I'd been a Christian for about four years and had become a youth worker. I loved my job. I liked being up front and, rightly or wrongly, being the one people liked. One evening I was out on the streets where I saw a gang of young lads getting themselves into trouble. I stopped and chatted with them. I wanted to get on their side, so in conversation I chose to swear, deliberately. I think I did it so that they would find it easier to accept me, and even to like me, but it backfired.

One of the lads asked me: 'You're a Christian, so how can you swear?' I tried to get out of it by saying that I was just as human as they were, but he was shocked. The others carried on with what they were doing but he wouldn't let it go.

It transpired that this guy had been watching me for a while: my lifestyle, what I said and where I went. Unbeknown to me, he was looking to me as a role model and was even considering becoming a Christian. I realised that by not being myself I had let myself, and this boy, down. Thankfully he still made the choice to become a Christian and we are friends even today, but this incident taught me a lesson. Now I'm careful to live wisely, watch my conversation and try to have the right response for everyone.

CHALLENGE

Find someone who will challenge you when you mess up. A friend is someone who knows everything about you, knows all your faults and still sticks with you. If you find someone you can be like this with, you will be less likely to falter.

MON 14 MAR

READ:
PROVERBS 27:10–17

KEY VERSE v17

'As iron sharpens iron, so one person sharpens another.'

I'M FORTUNATE ENOUGH to have one person I can call my best friend. She knows me so well that she sometimes finishes off my sentences for me. We laugh at the same thing when no one else gets it. When something is wrong she can see it in my face, she doesn't even need to ask me, she just knows. I'm well aware of how lucky I am. Not everyone has a friend like this. I only met her when I was 16 and, before then, I cannot say that I had a close relationship with anyone else.

Does this mean that my best friend agrees with everything I do or say? I wish! A good friend is not someone who necessarily agrees with everything I do and say; it's somebody who lovingly challenges me to be a better person. We grow in maturity when we can test our thoughts and ideas against another person, and when we're open to correction when we're wrong. My best friend is someone I can argue with but, at the end of the day, I know that she loves me and will stick with me.

THINK

Are you and your friends able to lovingly challenge one another to be better people? Are there people who could be friends like this to you? Look out for people like this and be willing to be this kind of friend yourself.

READ:
PROVERBS 27:1–6

KEY VERSE V6

'Wounds from a friend can be trusted'

I WAS GOING through a difficult time in my life and was straying from being a Christian. My friend told me that I knew what I was doing was wrong and I was justifying it by saying that God wanted me to do it. My friend was straight to the point in what she was saying. I reacted badly and for a while we were not on speaking terms. A couple of weeks went by during which we didn't have any contact at all. Then one morning when I was reading my Bible, today's key verse struck me.

My friend had hurt me with her words but, in doing this, she'd actually shown herself to be a true friend. She'd pointed out a vital area of my life that needed challenging. Isn't this what friendship is truly about? I thank God for her and now I put into action what she taught me about sincere friendship. Next time, I'll try not to react to a challenging comment from a friend but to listen, pray and seek God over what they say.

CHALLENGE

Perhaps your friends have been exactly what they were supposed to be: honest! For us to have true, vibrant, loving friendships there needs to be honesty. Challenge yourself to be more honest with your friends, in a loving way, this week.

WED 16 MAR

READ:
PROVERBS 17:1–10

KEY VERSE V9

'Whoever would foster love covers over an offence, but whoever repeats the matter separates close friends.'

THE WORLD AROUND us very rarely shows forgiveness. We see people and countries at war, politicians pulling each other down and newspapers taking any opportunity to destroy a celebrity's reputation. It's rare to see a glimpse of forgiveness when the finger is constantly being pointed at someone. However, I recall watching the news one evening and seeing a rare instance of a government minister seeking forgiveness. He said that he was sorry for atrocities that had been committed in his country and asked his people to forgive him.

Forgiveness is often difficult. At school I remember about ten friends in a room, all very angry with each other. The teacher and principal were both looking for a solution to the issue. Their suggestion was that we should all just make friends again. It's not always that simple. Forgiveness is not just a handshake and a 'Let's forget it'. Forgiveness is about acknowledging a fault but deliberately letting it go, rather than holding a grudge.

Dwelling on things destroys, letting go restores. People have faults – lots of them. But when we choose not to hold someone's faults against them, love prospers.

PRAY

Lord God, at times I get it wrong. I let You and my friends down. Help me to deal with any problems with my friends. Please forgive me and show me what it is to truly forgive others. Amen.

READ: MATTHEW 18:21–35

KEY VERSE v33

'Shouldn't you have had mercy on your fellow servant just as I had on you?'

THIS STORY JESUS tells shows a man who had different standards for different situations. In one situation he was the person who needed to be treated with generosity and so hoped to be treated with kindness. In the next situation he was asked to be the one to show kindness and generosity, but he did not act in this way. Instead of showing the kindness he'd been shown, he chose to treat his debtor harshly. So Jesus' challenge to us is clear: do we always treat others as we would hope to be treated?

Sometimes we can treat those closest to us the harshest! As we are familiar with them we can fall into the trap of thinking that it's OK to be hard on them, because they will forgive us. God teaches us that by acting in this way we will come to a sticky end. God has forgiven us a great deal, so we must be willing to show forgiveness to others, including our friends. If we need kindness from God, we should show the same kindness to other people.

PRAY

Lord God, help me to get things right with my friends. Help me to offer kindness and forgiveness to all of them, just as You have shown kindness and forgiveness to me. Amen.

FRI 18 MAR

READ: MATTHEW 5:43–48

KEY VERSE v47

'And if you greet only your own people, what are you doing more than others?'

HAVE YOU EVER written someone off just because of the way they looked or acted? I remember doing just that! I didn't want to pair up with another girl in class because I thought she looked different from me. She wasn't wearing fashionable clothes and her hair wasn't styled well. A couple of years later, I started a new class and got to sit next to her. We formed a great friendship, then one day she asked me about the time I didn't want to be her partner in a class. It was such a shock! I was really embarrassed because I hadn't realised that it had been her! I'd judged her without getting to know her.

We often pass up opportunities to connect with people because we assume that they're too different from us. But if we behave like this how are we different from people who don't know Jesus? Jesus welcomed and accepted everyone; including those other people didn't want to know. Following Jesus means doing what He did and choosing to show friendship – even to difficult and marginalised people. As we finish this series, remember that making friends doesn't mean forming a clique. It means showing Jesus' love and acceptance to people very different from ourselves.

THINK

How ready are you to show friendship to people who are different from you? Who might Jesus want you to befriend? Pray about this and ask Jesus to help you accept everyone, just as He does.

READ:
PROVERBS 19:16–21

KEY VERSE
V18

'Discipline your children, for in that there is hope'

PT2 DISCIPLINE

THINK OF A small child being taught to cross the road safely by an adult. No doubt we all had this kind of instruction when we were younger. But why? What is the purpose of teaching a child to cross the road with care? Surely it is to ensure that they stay safe and that, in time, they will be able to cross the road independently without fear of getting hurt.

CONTINUED»

CONTINUED

Discipline is about being taught to be wiser and more responsible. Most people, when they discipline us, do it for our own good (or at least that is their hope). They do it because they care about us and want the best for us. That doesn't stop us, however, from sometimes finding discipline hard to take. We like to think that we are pretty intelligent people who can do a good job looking out for ourselves. But those who love and care for us have a duty to look out for us, and to discipline us where necessary.

A blunt pencil is made sharper and regains its usefulness only by having bits shaved off. A rose bush can only continue to grow healthily and more beautifully when it is pruned. Sometimes, the process of being disciplined can be painful, and seems almost damaging. But it helps if we view this discipline differently: someone who cares about us is helping us to become the person we ultimately should be.

PRAY

Father God, please help me to respond positively to discipline and to see it as a way of growing. Help me to accept discipline graciously and willingly from those who love and care for me. Amen.

READ: JOHN 8:21–32

KEY VERSE v31

'Jesus said, "If you hold to my teaching, you are really my disciples."'

HAVE YOU NOTICED that the word 'discipline' is very similar to the word 'disciple'? Apparently, our word 'disciple' comes from the Latin for 'learner' and the word 'discipline' means 'instruction' or 'teaching'. To be a follower of Jesus is to follow and learn from His teachings. Or, to put it another way, to be a disciple of Jesus is to be subject to His discipline.

When we think of it in this way, discipline is not such a negative concept. Rather, it is something we should strive for. If we want to be genuine followers of Jesus, then we need to follow His teachings and instructions. We need to experience His discipline.

Today's Bible reading highlights that by being His disciples we can enjoy freedom as a result of knowing the truth (v32). We often think of discipline as something that limits us, stopping us from doing the things we would like to do. Over the next couple of weeks, we'll explore the idea that discipline actually helps us to be free.

THINK

In what ways do you think discipline might enable us to be freer? How might God discipline us?

TUES 22 MAR

READ:

PROVERBS 3:11–20

KEY VERSE v12

'the LORD disciplines those he loves, as a father the son he delights in.'

A COUPLE OF days ago we mentioned that parents usually discipline their children because they love them and want the best for them. We often talk of God as Father and, therefore, it's inevitable that God should have a role in disciplining us. Yet, for many of us, if we stop and think of God disciplining us, it can be hard to pinpoint what that actually involves. Does God punish us by striking us down with a dreadful illness or making it rain all day when we want it to be sunny? In reality, I suspect that this is not usually the case. However, the Bible assures us that God does indeed discipline us. But today's reading points out that this is because He loves us and we should not be unhappy about receiving His discipline.

Over the next few days we'll be thinking a bit more about what it means to be disciplined by God and what that discipline could look like.

PRAY

Thank You, Father, that You love us as Your children and want the best for us. Help us to accept Your discipline, as its purpose is for us to become better followers of You. Amen.

READ: 2 SAMUEL 12:1–12

KEY VERSE V11

'Out of your own household I am going to bring calamity on you.'

LET ME GIVE you a bit of background, in case you're not familiar with the story. King David had fallen for a woman who was already married. David slept with her, despite being well aware that this was wrong, and she became pregnant. In the end, David resorted to having her husband murdered, so that he could marry the woman and avoid a scandal.

In Nathan's story, which we read today, David is confronted with what he did. We need to face up to the truth when we do wrong. We need to admit what we have done and repent of it.

Although we can be forgiven by God when we sin, as Nathan tells David he has been, this does not free us from the negative consequences of what we've done. This is why learning to obey God and choosing well is so important.

How many times have you prayed something like this: 'God, I'm sorry. Please let everything go back to normal'? If God answered this prayer in the way I would like every time I prayed it, I do not believe that I would fully learn from my mistakes. It is only by facing up to the consequences, knowing that God loves and forgives us, that we are able to move on.

PRAY

Thank You, Father God, that You forgive us when we come to You in repentance. Help us to learn from the consequences of our mistakes. Amen.

THURS 24 MAR

READ:
MATTHEW 18:21–35

KEY VERSE V35

'This is how my heavenly Father will treat each of you unless you forgive your brother or sister from your heart.'

HAVE YOU EVER known a parent who seems to think that their children can do no wrong? Even if their children act rude or nasty, to their parents they are still little angels, perfect in every way. This is a good example of exactly why we need to have our mistakes pointed out to us and why we need to be disciplined.

Today's reading describes a man who behaved in a particularly nasty way. Despite the kindness shown to him in regard to his own debt, he refused to have mercy on someone who was in debt to him. And he was punished by being thrown into prison.

If we fail to show mercy and forgiveness towards others then we end up in a mess of anger and bitterness. God isn't cruel and doesn't 'torture' us Himself, but maybe He sometimes leaves us to the consequences of our actions to teach us – and make us more loving and forgiving. God is faithful to us, even though sometimes we are not faithful to Him. Whatever we have done wrong, He is prepared to forgive. If we have been given this grace, then we also have a responsibility to show the same grace to others.

CHALLENGE

Who was the last person who hurt you? Have you forgiven this person? Why not make a step to do so now?

READ:
1 PETER 1:3–9

KEY VERSE V7

'These have come so that the proven genuineness of your faith ... may result in praise, glory and honour'

ONE WAY IN which we can receive discipline and be made more into the people God wants us to be is by being allowed to go through difficult times. You may remember that last weekend we talked about the need for pencils to be sharpened and rose bushes to be pruned. If you were trying to purify a metal, such as gold, you would subject it to high temperatures. This would help you to refine it and to separate the impurities from the molten gold.

Today's verses tell us that our faith can be refined by going through trials. Today is Good Friday, the day we remember Jesus going to the cross to die for us. What a trial that must have been – to have to suffer so much when He did not deserve to. But what an amazing outcome it had. Jesus defeated death and restored humankind's relationship with God! So as you face trials in your life, remember this: Jesus understands and you will come out of the refining fire stronger and more mature than you were before.

THINK

How do you feel when you are going through a difficult time? Can you look back at times in your life that have been hard and see how God has strengthened you and brought you closer to Him through them?

WEEKEND

26/27 MAR [EASTER SUNDAY]

READ:
PROVERBS 5:1–14

KEY VERSE v12

'You will say, "How I hated discipline! How my heart spurned correction!"'

HOW DO YOU feel if you are told off in public? I can vividly remember a Victorian day at school as a child. I needed to leave part way through the school day to attend a medical appointment. My father had arranged with the teacher that he would come in, dressed as a Victorian headmaster, to collect me. I knew nothing of this arrangement. Later on during the day, my dad entered the room in his robes and proceeded to shout at me, insisting that I go with him to the headmaster's office. I was devastated. Not only had I been told off in front of all my classmates, but I hadn't even been doing anything wrong in the first place!

Not many of us like being disciplined, and we may be tempted to ignore those who try to set us straight. But try to imagine what might happen if we do not have our mistakes pointed out and made clear to us. Watching someone make bad decisions can be like watching a horrific crash in slow motion.

Today's reading highlights that those people who choose to ignore wise instruction usually live to regret it. As a child, my cousin was allowed to drink her juice from a wine glass at a special occasion. She insisted on holding the glass at the bottom of the stem, despite protests from her mother who told her that the glass would break. Sure enough, the glass did break and she was made to look silly for not following her mother's advice. If we don't pay attention to those who try to instruct us and discipline us, we run the risk of embarrassment or even public disgrace.

CHALLENGE

How do you respond to discipline? What might be the consequences if you choose to ignore those who try to help you by disciplining you?

READ:
PROVERBS 5:21–23

KEY VERSE v22

'The evil deeds of the wicked ensnare them; the cords of their sins hold them fast.'

WE MIGHT LONG to be free from rules that restrict us from doing what we want to do. Many people like to tell us that rules are there to be broken. But can you imagine a school without rules or a society with no laws?

Imagine that you and a group of your friends sailed off to a desert island and established a new community. Very quickly you would need to develop a set of rules in order to prevent chaos from reigning. What sort of laws might these be? And why is each of them so important?

In actual fact, being free from rules or laws does not lead to freedom, but chaos. If we are allowed to do what we want, then today's reading tells us that we become trapped and caught by our own wrongdoing. Rules protect us and help us to live our lives fully. Because we have laws and a police force to enforce those laws, we can go about our daily lives feeling secure. We are set free by the laws we have in place.

THINK

Think of those places where people do live in fear: perhaps a country with a corrupt police force or no clear/fair government in power. Pray that God would help to bring about a stable and fair government and set these people free.

READ: ROMANS 6:12–23

KEY VERSE v22

'But now that you have been set free from sin and have become slaves of God'

IF SOMEONE IS in authority over you, does it mean that you have to do everything they tell you to do? In most circumstances, probably not. We have free will and, as such, can decide whether or not to do what a parent, teacher or other person in authority asks us to do. However, we will face the consequences of any decision we take.

When I was a child, my father and I made a request on a radio show for a message to be read out and a song to be played for my mum and my brother. We did not want to tell them what we had done, but asked them to listen to the radio show. My mother duly did so, but my brother refused to listen, choosing instead to watch something on the television. As a consequence, he missed hearing the request and his name mentioned on the radio.

Sometimes, when we are too stubborn to do what someone who loves us asks us to do, we miss out on a possible good consequence. Today's Bible reading tells us that the reward for obeying God is eternal life. This is in contrast to the pain that results from being a slave to sin.

CHALLENGE

Is God calling you to do something in particular, or to give something up? Are you resisting Him in this? Take a brave step today and decide to obey Him. It might be scary, but it'll definitely be worth it.

WED 30 MAR

READ:
HEBREWS 12:1–13

KEY VERSE v10

'God disciplines us for our good, in order that we may share in his holiness.'

IN ORDER TO achieve anything in life, we often have to endure hardship along the way. For academic success, we need to study hard. To achieve sporting success, we need to be disciplined in our training.

Today's passage reminds us that the Christian life is not always easy. Sometimes we might even feel like giving up. Marathon runners talk about 'hitting the wall' when they feel as if they can go no further. However, when they keep on pushing past this wall of exhaustion, they are somehow able to go on. Today's passage tells us that when we feel like this, we should fix our eyes on Jesus and allow ourselves to be inspired by Him.

God isn't going to simply remove all the obstacles from our path and make our lives easy. We don't become Christians in order to have an easier life. However, when we are struggling, we should be assured that God is there with us as our coach. Unlike an earthly coach or father, God really does always know best. We really can trust in Him and His instructions for our life.

CHALLENGE

Today's reading talks about throwing off the things that hold us back such as sin. Is there anything that you think God, your coach, is calling you to throw off? Accept His discipline and instruction because He truly does know what is best for you.

READ: ROMANS 8:28–39

KEY VERSE v39

'neither height nor depth, nor anything else in all creation, will be able to separate us from the love of God'

IN ROMANS 8, Paul challenges us to see the big picture. As we reflected yesterday, during times of trouble it is so easy to think that God has abandoned us, and yet the Bible and history are full of stories that show how wrong that idea is.

Paul is clear that God doesn't always seem to help, but that 'God causes everything to work together'. So a situation might not be what we had hoped for or expected, but God is still very much in control. He causes things to happen so that we become more like Jesus, and we will see this process of sanctification (becoming holy, more like God) complete when we are glorified in heaven. The passage then goes on to highlight that suffering is not the end of the story, but is just a part of the story. God cares so much for us that He gave up Jesus. But through Jesus' suffering God was able to work for good.

When we are in the midst of a time of discipline or trial, we need to remember that God holds the bigger picture. He knows what He is doing. Are we prepared to put our trust in Him?

PRAY

Father God, help us in the midst of trouble, pain and suffering to see Your big picture, and to understand that victory is Yours and nothing in all creation will ever be able to separate us from Your love. Amen.

READ: 2 THESSALONIANS 3:6–13

KEY VERSE V9

'We did this ... in order to offer ourselves as a model for you to imitate.'

FOR MUCH OF the last fortnight, we have looked at our response to being disciplined ourselves. But this is only one side of the story. As we get older, we are increasingly faced with taking on the role of disciplining others and setting an example to younger people. Perhaps you help out with children's work at church, mentor a younger pupil at school or earn money through babysitting – or maybe you have younger brothers or sisters. Even if you can't think of a specific situation that is like one of the situations listed above, I have no doubt that some younger people, somewhere, look up to you in some way.

Today's reading gives some wise principles for all those of us involved in disciplining and setting an example to others. Are we doing it for the satisfaction of feeling powerful and exploiting people? Or are we exercising our authority in a godly way? Our motivation in leading and disciplining people should be to serve them, help them and give them a model of godly living for them to copy.

THINK

Think about the people who look up to you. How do you teach them, instruct them and help set them free to live wise and godly lives? After all, that's what the ultimate aim of discipling and discipline should be.

READ:

1 SAMUEL 15:10–29

KEY VERSE

V11

'I regret that I have made Saul king, because he has turned away from me and has not carried out my instructions.'

T★LENT PT2

I HAD A friend at college who was a very talented fencer. (By 'fencer', I mean he was good at the sport of fencing, not that he used to put up fences!) His sword hand moved too fast for his opponent to even see him move, let alone do anything about it. My friend seemed set for an international career in the sport. But then he discovered drugs and alcohol. When he'd got into the habit of indulging in these things, he was still a good fencer, but he wasn't brilliant anymore. The drugs had slowed down

CONTINUED▸▸

CONTINUED»

his reactions to the point where he was now beatable. His dreams of an international career were over.

Like my friend, Saul had started out so promisingly. He was tall, handsome and influential; every inch a king (see 1 Sam. 9). People probably wouldn't have been surprised when God chose Saul as King of Israel. But somewhere along the line, Saul got complacent. He started thinking that he could ignore God, do what he wanted and rule Israel in the way he thought was right. My friend thought he could meddle with drugs and still be an international fencer. Saul thought he could stop listening to God and still be king. Both were wrong. God rejected Saul as king, not because Saul wasn't talented, but because he was ignoring God. Our skill and talent in themselves aren't what matter. What really matters is our attitude. As we use our talents, are we obeying God? Or are we getting complacent and just doing what we want?

PRAY

Ask God to help you see whether your attitude towards Him is right. If you know you haven't been obeying God in something, now would be a good time to repent of that. Commit to listening to God and obeying Him in everything.

READ: JUDGES 16:4–22

KEY VERSE V17

'So he told her everything. "No razor has ever been used on my head"'

IT'S EASY FOR our talent to go to our head, and this story is one of that happening a bit too literally. Samson had been given superhuman strength from God, but in one of those Old Testament twists, the degree of this strength was indelibly linked to the length of Samson's hair. Samson was told this and as he listens to God and keeps his hair on, he is used by God in amazing ways. He knew that if anyone found out where his strength came from, he would be in a whole heap of trouble.

But Samson began to rely on himself, and left God out of the picture. Eventually he let his secret slip to a woman working for Israel's enemies, the Philistines. Unsurprisingly, he wakes up one morning to find a colder head, and the start of his downfall.

Samson was doing fine. His talent was being used well, until he started relying on himself and thinking he didn't need God's help. It's in these moments, when we begin to think too much of ourselves, that we are at our most vulnerable. For our talent to be used to its full potential we need to remember where it came from. Because if our talent goes to our heads, it could end up costing us our hair!

PRAY

Ask God for humility, to keep you relying on Him, rather than getting proud and trusting your own talent to get you through.

TUES 5 APR

READ:
JUDGES 6:11–24

KEY VERSE V15

'how can I save Israel? My clan is the weakest in Manasseh, and I am the least in my family.'

GIDEON DIDN'T THINK he had what it took to be a leader. This possibility was so far from what he was expecting that he kept testing God just to make sure this was actually coming from Him. You can read what happened next for yourself, but after a series of odd events he ended up leading Israel to one of their greatest military victories. He never saw it coming.

The Bible is full of people being used when they least expect it. Jonah was a reluctant prophet who saved a city, Moses had a stutter and Peter was a lowly fisherman who went on to lead the Early Church. God worked through these people when they least expected it, unearthing talents they didn't know they had. He does the same today. God may not be asking you to lead the Israelite army, but there are amazing plans and talents for you, perhaps where you least expect them. So you've got to be open to whatever God has for you to do! Often when we move out of where we are comfortable, we rely on God and He can use us in more exciting ways than we could possibly imagine.

CHALLENGE

It's time to get out of your comfort zone! Ask God to lead you and to work through you in unexpected ways this week.

READ:
LUKE 9:37–43

KEY VERSE V40

'I begged your disciples to drive it out, but they could not.'

JAMES, THE INVENTOR, was a failure. He had a great idea but he just couldn't quite get it right. Every time he would change one thing, something else would go wrong. But he believed he had something worth sticking at. He learnt from each attempt and kept going. Eventually he had amassed 5,126 failed attempts. But number 5,127 was to be a success. The man's invention? A particular type of vacuum cleaner. His name? James Dyson. If it weren't for all those failures, we wouldn't have those clever bag-less machines that we have today. Failure was vital to help James learn.

In this story some disciples came back to Jesus saying that things hadn't gone how they'd expected; that they'd failed. Did Jesus cast them off as failures? No. He helped them to learn from the experience. Those disciples didn't let their failure define them. In fact, once Jesus' time on earth had come to an end it was these disciples who started the spread of the gospel across the entire world. Talent doesn't come pre-packaged for success. We will fail at times. But if we learn from this and move on, great things can still happen.

THINK

Have you failed at something recently? What have you learnt from it? Do you shy away from situations where you might fail? Have the courage to try, fail and learn.

THURS 7 APR

READ:
LUKE 10:1–20

KEY VERSE v17

'The seventy-two returned with joy and said, "Lord, even the demons submit to us in your name."'

FORTUNATELY, WE NO longer live in a society where our worth comes from how handy we are with a sword, but if it did, I'd want to know if I was any good before Sir Sword-fighty-a-lot challenged me to a duel. Unfortunately, sometimes you'll only learn if you're good at something by trying it.

I love the model Jesus uses here. The disciples have been hanging round with Him for a while, seeing the way He operates. So when their time comes, does He ease them into the work? Oh no. He sends them out into the world, on their own. Terrifying, eh? As much as it was a risk for the disciples to try this stuff, it was equally risky for Jesus – He had a reputation to maintain! He sent His followers off with a few words of advice (about dust and wiping their feet, oddly). They learnt what they could do by doing it. They didn't get everything right, but they learnt a lot more than they would have done by just watching Jesus do it.

So go on, take a risk. Try something different. You'll never know if you can do it if you don't give it a go.

CHALLENGE

That thing you've been thinking about for ages, worrying that you wouldn't be able to do it, putting off in case it doesn't go well. Do it. Right now!

FRI 8 APR

READ: 1 KINGS 3:16–28

KEY VERSE v28

'When all Israel heard the verdict the king had given, they held the king in awe, because they saw that he had wisdom from God'

LAST WEEKEND, WE looked at the tragic end of Saul's rule over Israel. Saul was talented, but blew it simply by ignoring God. Two generations on, we see a turning point in Solomon's life in 1 Kings 3. Solomon wasn't like his predecessor. He relied on God to make him a good king and prayed for God's wisdom to help him lead Israel (1 Kings 3:3–14).

In verses 16–28, we see an example of Solomon's impressive wisdom in action. Wisdom is a fantastic talent to have. It can have a dramatic impact on the people around us, as it did for the women who came to Solomon. Solomon himself urges us to get wise, whatever else we do (Prov. 4:7).

And in the New Testament, James assures us that God's wisdom is available to any of us if we just ask (James 1:5). We can ask God for wisdom, just as Solomon did, and be confident that we will receive it. We can then use God's wisdom to help and influence the people around us.

THINK

However wise you think you are already, ask God to give you His wisdom. Then use that wisdom to help the people around you in a godly way.

WEEKEND

9/10 APR

READ:
ACTS 9:36–43

KEY VERSE v40

'Turning towards the dead woman, he said, "Tabitha, get up." She opened her eyes, and seeing Peter she sat up.'

WE BEGAN THE second section of our series on talent with a few examples of people using their talents to spectacular effect. But actually, today's example is a bit different. It's not quite accurate to call Peter's ability to heal a 'talent'. This isn't a natural ability, but a supernatural one. (A while ago, we mentioned the difference between a talent and a spiritual gift and this is an example of that difference.)

Nobody is naturally a healer. Many people are naturally caring and compassionate, but nobody can heal anyone like this without the power of God. At times, God works through an individual to heal another individual, but this actually has very little to do with the natural talents of either person. This kind of healing is nothing less than the power of God working through a human being.

Knowing that we're unable to heal anyone shouldn't be discouraging; it should be liberating and comforting. We can pray for someone who's sick, knowing that the results aren't up to us. God is the One who will take care of that. Although none of us have a natural talent for healing, God might still use us as His agents for healing others. This should inspire us to keep praying for people we know who are sick. It's risky to pray for this kind of thing. For whatever reason, God might not heal the person we're praying for. But our chances of seeing someone healed are considerably higher if we bother praying!

PRAY

Who do you know who is sick? Pray for that person and ask God to heal them. Also, listen to what God might have to say about His plans for this person. If He doesn't heal them immediately, what else might He be doing for them?

MON 11 APR

READ:
PHILEMON 4–7

KEY VERSE v7

'Your love has given me great joy and encouragement, because you ... have refreshed the hearts of the Lord's people.'

NOT ALL TALENTS are obvious and spectacular. People who are confident, outgoing and seem comfortable on a stage get a lot of attention, but often it's the quieter ones who make a real difference; the ones who are talented in helping and caring for other people and quietly committed to doing just that.

The church leader Howard Hendricks once said: 'You can impress people from a distance but you can only impact them up close.' Don't make the mistake of thinking you have to be loud and outgoing to do anything significant. You might be talented in showing kindness to people in a way that 'refreshes their hearts'. Using that talent can make a huge difference to someone who needs encouragement and comfort. Even Paul, possibly the most influential church leader and teacher who ever lived, needed the encouragement that someone like Philemon could give him. If you know that's a talent you have, please use it! Keep in mind the enormous difference it can make. And if you're not sure whether you have this talent, give it a try!

THINK

How can you refresh the hearts of God's people? Whether or not you think you're talented in caring for other people, ask for God's help in this.

READ: 1 SAMUEL 16:1–13

TUES 12 APR

KEY VERSE v7

'The LORD does not look at the things people look at. People look at the outward appearance, but the LORD looks at the heart.'

IT'S AMAZING THE way talent affects how we look at someone. We all remember Susan Boyle coming on stage on *Britain's Got Talent* and being blown away by her voice. But this was only after we judged her for how she looked. How depressing is that? The whole country assumed this woman wasn't anything special, because she looked slightly odd.

Yes, talent is important. God has given us all different things we can do. But we must balance that with the fact that our talent doesn't make us any more valuable. Susan Boyle is loved by God whether Simon Cowell liked her voice or not!

David didn't look like anything special either, but God loved him, chose him and had big plans for him anyway.

God's love for us is unconditional. It does not depend on whether we can sing well on a stage in front of some cameras. Your talent doesn't define you any more than your haircut or where you went on holiday last summer. So we shouldn't judge someone else because of their talent, any more than we should because of their appearance.

CHALLENGE

Think about how you treat people. Is it based on what the world says about them or the way God looks at them? Choose to love and accept the people around you, regardless of their talent, just as God does.

WED 13 APR

READ:
PROVERBS 22:17–29

KEY VERSE v29

'Do you see someone skilled in their work? They will serve before kings; they will not serve before officials of low rank.'

HAVE YOU EVER discovered a band you love but no one else seems to have heard of their music? Have you then seen that band become massively famous? That's happened to me once or twice. It brings a strange mixture of emotions. There's an element of pride that I found this band before my friends did and a tinge of jealousy that these guys are everywhere now when they used to be my secret! More than anything, though, when something like this happens, you're delighted that people so talented are getting the recognition they deserve.

Someone with talent deserves to have that talent noticed. Fortunately, most of the time, talent does get noticed, but that isn't guaranteed. So if you see someone with obvious talent, it's great to help other people see that talent too. Look around you. Who has real talent? How can you encourage them to use that talent to honour God?

PRAY

Pray for particular people you know who have clear talents. Ask God to help them hone their talents and use them for His glory. And look out for opportunities to encourage each of these people.

READ:
ACTS 9:19–31

KEY VERSES vv26–27

'[Saul] tried to join the disciples, but they were all afraid of him ... But Barnabas took him and brought him to the apostles.'

WHEN I MET Ryan, he was 15. I'd been asked to run a new group for 11–14s in our church, and I knew we needed leaders. Someone suggested I could get Ryan involved. I didn't know him very well but decided to take a chance on him. The first couple of times the group met, Ryan looked like a rabbit in the headlights. But slowly, he began to feel more comfortable as a leader and the young people in the group responded well to him. Gradually, Ryan became one of the most reliable and helpful leaders I worked with. Fast forward ten years and Ryan is now at Bible college, finishing his PhD in theology. Much as I'd love to take the credit for this, I know it's all down to God making the most of the talents He gave Ryan in the first place. I'm just glad I gave Ryan a chance when I could.

Saul probably didn't look very promising either. He had a reputation for not just disliking Christians, but having them killed! However, Barnabas saw potential in Saul, chose to believe he had changed and took a chance on him, even though that involved a big risk. As we near the end of this series of readings, I pray that we will become people who not only use our own talents but celebrate the talents of others, even when that involves a risk.

CHALLENGE

Who do you know who has a clear talent? How can you help them use and develop that talent? Look for an opportunity today.

FRI 15 APR

READ:
LUKE 5:1–11

KEY VERSE v10

'Jesus said to Simon, "Don't be afraid; from now on you will fish for people."'

MY NEW YEAR'S resolution this year was to learn to play the accordion. I'm not musical at all. But this old accordion has been sitting in my parents' house for as long as I can remember. It originally belonged to some distant relative, but now it sits there, waiting to be used. I was sick of seeing that wasted potential. I wanted to do something about it.

Sometimes a person's talents lie there, untapped, waiting to be used. We need to unearth those talents. Jesus has an amazing ability to spot potential where no one else does. Just look at His disciples: the fishermen, the tax collectors, the religious nutters, the ones the rest of society had given up on. He took them off the shelf and turned them into a bunch of people ready to change the face of the world. Jesus brought out the best in these people, even when no one else knew it was there.

We can do the same. Look for the talent in the people around you. Once you've found it, do everything you can to encourage these people and nurture their talents. Could you mentor a younger person, for example? Help that person discover their talents, hone them and use them for God's kingdom. Don't let those talents sit in a room and get covered in dust.

THINK

What potential can you see in the people around you? How can you invest in someone and help them discover and use their talents?

READ:
JOB 38:1–18

KEY VERSE
V4

'Where were you when I laid the earth's foundation? Tell me, if you understand.'

PT3
THE TRINITY

HERE WE ARE, our third and final look at the Holy Trinity! In this last section we're going to think about God being the beginning and the end – that is, being present before the beginning of time and always being there forever into eternity.

Over the next few days we're going to be looking at what the Bible says about the creation of the world.

Today's verses are brilliant for helping us to understand our Creator God; the God who made the

CONTINUED

CONTINUED

seas and oceans (v8), gave orders to the morning (v12), and knows every part of the vast expanse of the earth (v18). (Read the rest of the chapter to see what else our amazing God created!)

This Holy Trinity is the Creator and Sustainer of the universe and of life itself, in all its complexity and detail – from the vastness of our galaxy to the absurdity of a jellyfish. The Holy Trinity is present throughout creation. Right from the beginning, our Triune God worked in relationship at making the world, and even today we can marvel at God's fingerprints on creation.

Just putting this chapter of the Bible into context, Job was a man who didn't have an easy life, to say the least. And during the first 37 chapters of this Bible book we see Job debating and arguing with his friends and being annoyed with God. Then comes this amazing chapter. The Lord finally has His turn to speak ... and it's enough to knock your socks off! Our God is undoubtedly powerful and in control. Instead of letting life get to us, let's take our problems to God, who created all life!

CHALLENGE

Look around outside today and take notice of God's creation. Admire it! This Holy Trinity we worship is always at work, within and throughout creation.

READ: GENESIS 1:1–5

KEY VERSE V2

'the Spirit of God was hovering over the waters.'

HAVE YOU EVER had the feeling that you have been there at the very beginning of something? Maybe a new footballer at your local club is breaking through into the first team and you just know he's going all the way to the England team. Maybe you've been to a gig and the support act is so good you know that before long they will also be huge.

Here, the Holy Spirit is present at the very dawn of time; before the creation of the world, before Jesus is born a human thousands of years later and before the disciples nervously wait in the upper room after Jesus' resurrection and ascension. The Spirit of God is present throughout creation, and exists inside and outside of time itself. Big stuff!

God speaks and the world is created. Have you ever wondered who He was talking to in verse 3? The Trinity is a relational God. The three Persons of the Trinity are talking to each other, discussing what is needed for life to exist on the planet they've made. The Spirit of God is the life force of creation that, together with the Father and the Son, upholds all things in existence.

PRAY

Thank You, Lord, that You were present – Father, Son and Holy Spirit – at the creation of the world. Thank You that You are a relational God who longs to be my Friend and to draw me deeper into Your mysterious and awesome love and power. Amen.

READ:
JOHN 1:1–5

KEY VERSE V3

'Through him all things were made; without him nothing was made that has been made.'

WE'VE LOOKED SO far at the Spirit's involvement in creation. Now we shift our focus to Jesus' part to play. John writes that the Word (Jesus) was with God and was God; an amazing and really helpful glimpse of the Trinity; a Triune God deciding to make everything through the Son.

Jesus gave life to everything that was created. By the Son's life, light came into the world. Jesus goes on to tell His disciples that He is 'the light of the world' (John 8:12) and interestingly Genesis tells us that on the first day of creation God said, 'Let there be light' (Gen. 1:3).

Here we see a Creator God, fully involved, with sleeves rolled up and hands dirty, shaping the universe. I once worked in the kitchen of a very posh restaurant in London. Without the head chef's say-so, no dish was allowed out of the kitchen, because his reputation was on the line with every meal that was served. Sloppy work was certainly not tolerated. Like this perfectionist chef, nothing but perfection was going to be served up by God. Because the Trinity is perfect, God's plan for creation was perfect: through the Son a perfect universe was created by God.

THINK

Are you currently facing any situations that are in need of Jesus' perfect light shining into them? Talk to Jesus now.

READ: ISAIAH 53:1–6

KEY VERSE V3

'He was despised and rejected by mankind, a man of suffering, and familiar with pain.'

WE MOVE ON from looking at the Trinity and creation, to exploring the Old Testament prophecies of Jesus coming to earth as the second Person of the Trinity.

To show the world that He is the beginning and the end, God gave many people in the Bible visions of the future – things that had not yet happened.

Today we read Isaiah's prophecy, which details the events of Jesus' life and death, hundreds of years before they even came to pass.

Jesus fulfils this prophecy, and many others, within the details of His earthly life: the town in which He is born, His escape to Egypt, His heart for the poor and sick, the type of death He suffers and, ultimately, His resurrection.

God uses Isaiah's words to affect not only his contemporaries, but also many others in future generations. We can marvel at the amazing foresight Isaiah was given and know that our God always sees what's next!

CHALLENGE

Why not spend some time today reading a few Old Testament prophecies and note how they are later fulfilled in the Gospels (eg Isa. 40:3 and Matt. 3:1–3; Micah 5:2 and Matt. 2:1–6; Psa. 41:9 and Matt. 26:20–23,47–49).

THURS 21 APR

READ:
GENESIS 32:22–32

KEY VERSE v24

'So Jacob was left alone, and a man wrestled with him till daybreak.'

DO YOU KNOW the meaning of your name? Do you think your parents chose your name because of its meaning or because they liked the sound of it? During Bible times the choice of a name was very important. It identified more than just a nice-sounding name – rather it defined your character and temperament.

Jacob means 'deceiver' and, even before he was born, Jacob wrestled with his elder twin for his future inheritance. He goes on, later in the story, to deceive his own father and, in turn, is later deceived by his own father-in-law. Then what happens? Well, further on in his life, when Jacob takes his whole family away from his crafty father-in-law, Jacob has a very interesting wrestling match one night with a man. Yet is He just a man?

What man can bless unless that man is God? What man changes a person's name and identity (Jacob to Israel) unless that man is God? If Jesus is God in bodily form (Col. 2:9), then when God appeared to people during the Old Testament, this was as one member of the Holy Trinity. These mysterious appearances often hint at this member possibly being the Son – not yet come to earth.

PRAY

Thank You, Jesus, that You are involved in the lives of Your people. Thank You that before You were born in Bethlehem, You may have appeared in the form of man to key characters at key times to help Your nation of Israel grow. Amen.

READ: GENESIS 18:1–20

KEY VERSE v2

'Abraham looked up and saw three men standing nearby.'

THE TRINITY IS not a modern concept, but is very biblical, appearing way back in Genesis, the first book of the Bible. We have seen how Jesus appeared in bodily form (often in the guise of an angel messenger) to individuals in the Old Testament. And today, in Genesis, we read that the Lord appeared to Abraham. This time, God appears as one of three men. The Bible is quite specific in the number of men who appeared and Abraham even asked Sarah for three bowls to feed them (v6). Yet the Bible tells us several times that it is the Lord who speaks (eg vv13,17,20).

The Lord appears, speaks and prophesies the birth of Isaac (v10), yet the description is of three men. Did the Lord appear together with two angels? Whatever happened, we can be sure that the Triune God is present in the world and at work before the birth of Isaac and the creation of the nation of Israel. He was and always is there.

THINK

Have you ever encountered God for yourself? Maybe you've felt the Holy Spirit's presence or have heard God speak to you (audibly or to your heart). Ask God to show Himself to you in some way today.

WEEKEND
23/24 APR

READ:
REVELATION 1:1–8

KEY VERSE V8

'I am the Alpha and the Omega ... who is, and who was, and who is to come'

HOW DO YOU describe God? What words can adequately do justice to our awesome, Almighty God? No human could even *try* unless God Himself had revealed Himself to that person and then given him the words!

In the beginning of the book of Revelation, John uses time to describe God, calling Him the God who always was and who is and who is still to come. This description shouts aloud the timelessness of God. We've previously read about how He was even there before the beginning of time as we know it!

Time is a limitation that we, as humans, are constrained by: time for bed, time for school etc. We age and feel the effects of time. We sometimes feel like we just don't have enough time in the day! However, as we see from John's description, we serve a God who is not constrained by time, but instead rules over it with power.

Another similar description of God, used by John in Revelation, is that He is the Alpha and Omega – the beginning and the end. Our great and glorious God rules as the Trinity over time and space.

John describes this Triune God in verses 4 to 8. The amazing revelation John received is written down for us and describes God in a series of visual ways. Go back and read it again! What a mighty Trinitarian picture! He is the God of all time, the Father, Son and Holy Spirit.

PRAY

Father, thank You for Your revelation to us of Your mighty power and awesome might. Thank You that You are the God of space and time, that You even broke into time as God the Son and raised Him from the dead by the power of God the Spirit. Amen.

MON 25 APR

READ: REVELATION 5:1–14

KEY VERSE V6

'Then I saw a Lamb, looking as if it had been slain, standing at the centre of the throne'

ON A SPORTING front, some nations regularly experience defeat. Many of us have seen our national football team, heads down, stumbling towards the dressing room with dejected and humiliated looks on their faces. The whole nation groans as, yet again, the expectancy of winning a tournament is not realised.

Here, in the book of Revelation, John describes to us the scene in heaven. The scrolls are about to be opened, yet there is no one found among all the people present who is worthy of this highly-esteemed task. Then the scene focuses on a Lamb, looking as if it had been slaughtered.

This description of Jesus is in huge contrast to yesterday's great and mighty God described by John. Here we see a slaughtered lamb – the image of an obedient Son and a murdered member of the Trinity. Yet the Triune God allows this to happen in order to save humankind from its sin.

We close this chapter with the whole of heaven joining together in worship for the Lamb that was slain. The revelation of the plan of the Trinity should, like this scene in Revelation, cause us to stand in awe and worship of the God who rescued us.

THINK

Take time out to reread these verses and use them to enable you to worship God, as you reflect on the great plan of the Trinity to rescue us from sin and death.

READ: PSALM 2:1–12

KEY VERSE V4

'The One enthroned in heaven laughs;
the Lord scoffs at them.'

HOW MANY PEOPLE do you think have a wrong image of God? Perhaps they see God as an old man in heaven, all dressed in white, yet somehow very distant from planet Earth. Or maybe they see Him as a tubby 'Santa-type' God who will let sins go unpunished at the end of time because He is just gentle and kind. Or others possibly see Him as a vindictive God who reaches down from heaven with a big stick, hurting people just for the sake of His own entertainment.

According to the psalmist, God fits none of the above images but is very different altogether. The Lord Almighty, this mysterious Triune God, is a God who laughs at human plans that attempt to oppose His mighty purposes.

Psalm 2 teaches us that God is sovereign. He is King. The Trinity reigns! The great Trinitarian plan of salvation – set into motion at Jesus' birth – will one day come to completion when all who love God are gathered to be with Him forever. No ruler, no power, no politician, no authority, no army or weapon will ever stop the saving plan of the Trinity being worked out on earth.

THINK

Which image of God do we have in our minds when we make our plans for the future? Are we under the illusion that 'you make your own luck in this world' or are we laying our lives down before the King, asking Him to shape their course?

WED 27 APR

READ:
REVELATION 20:11–15

KEY VERSE v12

'The dead were judged according to what they had done as recorded in the books.'

TODAY WE FOCUS in on the Father, whose role for the end of time is to judge all. The Father sits on the throne to judge fairly all the injustice that has ever taken place in the world – all the pain and sorrow, war and suffering that has been caused to humanity by humanity. Even death itself is finally judged and punished.

The great master plan of the Trinity now ends with this scene. Jesus has beaten death and sin. The enemy of the Church, Satan, is defeated and the Church has, through the power of the Spirit, increased through the centuries, bringing many people to believe the truth of the gospel message. Finally, the Father has His say.

The image of hell is not a popular one in today's churches but Jesus spoke more about hell than anyone else in the Bible. As those with a living, breathing friendship with the Holy Trinity, we now have nothing to fear in this life or the next, for we have been won forever through the saving work of the Father, Son and Holy Spirit.

CHALLENGE

One day, everyone will be judged for what they have done with the life God gave them. Think about this. How does it make you feel towards reaching those who don't know Jesus? How does it make you feel about the injustice you see around you in your life or in the world?

READ: ISAIAH 6:1–8

KEY VERSE V3

'Holy, holy, holy is the LORD Almighty; the whole earth is full of his glory.'

WHY DO WE use repetition? It's everywhere! 'Location, location, location' or 'Mind the gap. Mind the gap'. Is it just to show its importance or to drum into us a particular kind of message?

Isaiah is given this wonderful vision of heaven, with the Lord seated on a throne and the angels surrounding Him. All of heaven shouts 'Holy, holy, holy'. Is the word 'Holy' repeated because God is so holy and as humans we need to understand this, or is it repeated because God is, in fact, three in one – the mystery that is the Trinity?

The one place where we will understand the Trinity more easily will be in heaven. We will be in perfect relationship with God and we'll see, sense and know our Triune God for ourselves. Can you imagine the scene in heaven: God seated on the throne, the angels singing, and YOU there too? As Christians on earth now, we are caught up in the mystery of the Trinity; in heaven we will be amazed at the majesty of the Trinity. All seeds of doubt will vanish when we are faced with the sovereignty and glory of God.

PRAY

Lord, thank You that one day we will no longer struggle to understand the Trinity, but we will actually see with our own eyes the majesty and sovereignty of our Triune God. Amen.

FRI 29 APR

READ: PHILIPPIANS 2:5–11

KEY VERSE V10

'that at the name of Jesus every knee should bow, in heaven and on earth and under the earth'

DO YOU LOOK forward to things? Maybe the summer holidays or a nice birthday treat? Perhaps an upcoming film or a local cup match for your favourite team? We all look forward to things in our lives and long for these moments to come.

In the same way, our Triune God looks forward to the day when we will be with Him in heaven forever and the great Trinitarian plan to rescue the human race is finally fulfilled. In writing to the Philippians, Paul tells us that 'at the name of Jesus every knee should bow'. When we are faced with this glorious God and go to be with Him forever, we will be brought to our knees in wonder, awe and joy.

This scene will be better than any church service, celebration, worship conference or festival we go to – it will be worship like no other. We will see God in all His glory and this will cause us to sing and praise Him, surrounded by angels and fellow believers. We will be caught up in perfect worship of our Triune God.

CHALLENGE

The Trinity has placed the name of Jesus, the Son, as the highest name in all existence. How much do you value the name of Jesus? Think about what a wonderful name this is and how you can bring honour to it by how you live your life.

WEEKEND
30 APR

READ:
PSALM 86:1–10

KEY VERSE V8

'Among the gods there is none like you, Lord; no deeds can compare with yours.'

WE'VE COME TO the end of this issue of *Mettle* and our look at the Trinity! Today let's conclude what we've learnt and heard of our three-in-one God by briefly looking at how other gods compare with Him.

So how does our Triune God compare with the gods of other world religions? How different is our Trinitarian God to the god of the Muslims or the many gods of the Hindus, or the Buddhists?

The psalmist declares that our Triune God is completely different from all world religions, faiths and values. He calls on the Lord to hear him

CONTINUED

CONTINUED

and answer him. This is a God who is interested in his life; a relational God who is kind and forgiving.

In Buddhism, we see a human religious philosophy; in Hinduism, a religion that worships thousands of gods. In Islam and Judaism we learn of two religions that worship only one God, not the Triune God of Christianity.

We don't worship a God who demands things of us, but one who respects our choice and offers His friendship and forgiveness freely. He is a God who understands everything we experience because He made it all and walked the earth Himself as a man.

We hope that this study on the Trinity has given you a hunger to go deeper in your understanding of this awesome God we worship and become closer to Him, day by day.

CHALLENGE

Write down some key points you've learnt during this study of the Trinity and practise some questions and answers with your Christian friends. This will help prepare you for when you talk to someone who wants to know more about God. If there are any questions you are still unsure of, talk to a leader at church!

NOTES

ORDER FORM

4 EASY WAYS TO ORDER:

1. For credit/debit card payment, call 01252 784700 (Mon–Fri, 9.30am – 5pm)
2. Visit our online store at www.cwr.org.uk/store
3. Send this form together with a cheque made payable to CWR to: CWR, Waverley Abbey House, Waverley Lane, Farnham, Surrey GU9 8EP
4. Visit a Christian bookshop

YOUR DETAILS
Name:
CWR ID No. (if known):
Address:
Postcode:
Telephone No. (for queries):
Email:

SUBSCRIPTIONS (NON DIRECT DEBIT)	QTY	PRICE (INCLUDING P&P)			TOTAL
		UK	Europe	Elsewhere	
Mettle (1yr, 3 issues)*		£14.50	£16.60	£18.75*	
(Subscription prices already include postage and packing)				**TOTAL** **B**	

Please circle which four-month issue you would like your subscription to commence from:

Jan–Apr	**May–Aug**	**Sep–Dec**

*Order direct from CWR or from your National Distributor. For a full list of our National Distributors and contact details, visit www.cwr.org.uk/distributors

Mettle is also available as a Digital Edition, for more information visit **www.mettleapp.org.uk**